MY DISABILITY DOESN'T DEFINE ME

. . . .

Louis A. Vendetti

D1249320

Cover design by Rob Williams of ILoveMyCover.com and William Ross, Graphic Design Student, Hudson Valley Community College

Edited by Qat Wanders of Wandering Words Media
Formatted by Wild Words Formatting
Headshot on cover taken by Saratoga Portrait Studio
Photographer Dave Bigler

ISBN-13: 978-1-732293205

This book is dedicated to Sean Craig.
Thank you for reminding me that, with a little
determination and hard work, anything
is possible. Rest in Peace, my friend.

This book is dedicated to Paul Moylan.
Thank you for guiding me through school
and through life. Rest in Peace, my friend.

TABLE OF CONTENTS

Foreword

by Andrew J. Matonak, Ed.D.,
Hudson Valley Community
College President

One of the most rewarding things about being a college president is the opportunity to meet exceptional, highly motivated students and learn about their stories — what makes them want to succeed, and what kinds of challenges they've met along the way. Each person's journey is unique, and each is significant in its own way. This book is a collection of stories from a student whose personal challenges have only made him more exceptional and motivated him to work harder. They are stories of persistence and success.

I met Louis Vendetti during the beginning of his time at Hudson Valley, and watching him continue to strive toward his educational goals has been extremely gratifying for me. Those of us who met Louis on campus immediately recognized him as an ambitious young man and a role model for other students. His tireless drive and spirit of self-improvement are infectious. He has a long history of inspiring those around him to push themselves to do better than they thought possible, and to overcome whatever obstacles life puts before them, regardless of how long it takes or how many battles must be fought to get there. The book is a testament to that.

Now, I'm very proud to say that the influence of Louis' passion and strength of character isn't limited to those who meet him in person; anyone who picks up this book will be inspired by his tenacity and perhaps be reminded not to give up on their own dreams for the future.

As Hudson Valley's president, I consider it an honor to have students like Louis with us on campus. In fact, the college takes great pride in serving more than seven hundred students with disabilities each year. Our job is to ensure that they receive every opportunity and resource they may need to reach their personal, academic, and career goals. They're a critically important part of the fabric of our community. And year after year, they inspire us with everything they achieve. Louis is no exception.

His stories remind all of us that with hard work, determination, and an attitude that it's never an option to give up, we can each accomplish what we have set out to do and become what we have dreamed of, no matter the obstacles before us.

Enjoy this book, and next time you find yourself facing a challenge, just think: What would Louis do?

INTRODUCTION

by Karen Vendetti

When Lou told me he was writing a book about his life, I was not surprised as he has been writing stories since he could write. When he asked me to write the introduction for his book, I didn't know where to start; a thousand memories flooded back of our lives over the years: His triumph of winning a gold medal at the Empire Games and his disappointment when he got up the courage to ask a girl to be his girlfriend and she said no. What is the best way to introduce you to my son? I will tell you a little about his beginning.

Lou and his twin sister, Loren, were born at twenty-five week's gestation and were in the Neonatal Intensive Care Unit (NICU) for ninety-one days. Lou was baptized and given Last Rites before he was three days old as we did not know if he was going to live. He and his sister are our miracle babies. Lou developed hydrocephalus and had a shunt put in. Over the years, he has had multiple surgeries to replace shunts that have stopped working.

The kids were referred to early intervention and thus began our journey with doctors and therapists. We were told Lou had a 95% chance of having Cerebral Palsy. At the age of three, he was officially given that diagnosis, specifically Spastic Diplegia.

Lou has had physical therapy since he was six months old. The therapist came to the house three times a week to stretch his muscles and improve his range of motion. At first, his feet were put into casts to stretch his Achilles and eventually, he went into braces. He began walking with a posterior walker.

Lou loved talking to everyone he saw and when we went out in public he would flirt with every woman whose eye he could catch. Kids would stare and want to know what was wrong with him. Their mothers would tell them to stop staring and pull them away. One day, I brought Lou up to a young boy who was staring and told him to ask Lou about himself; that he would tell him. So Lou did. He said to the little boy, "My legs have Cerebral Palsy." I couldn't believe it! He didn't really understand what he said, but with those five words, he was declaring that Cerebral Palsy did not define him. He was right and that is how he lives his life.

PART I

. . . .

MY EARLY SCHOOLING

MY ELEMENTARY
SCHOOL YEARS

In the years leading up to college, I went to preschool, kindergarten, elementary school, middle school, and high school like all kids — but I was different — I had a physical disability that required me to use forearm crutches, a walker (when I was younger), and a manual wheelchair for long distance journeys. Due to safety reasons, I always knew I had a one-on-one aide, but I didn't know anything about my Individualized Education Plan (IEP) or the accommodations that it bestowed upon me — I just knew that I had to have an adult with me every minute of every day while in school — whether it be in class or transitions from class to class or from the bus into the school. At that time in my life, I didn't even know that the person in charge of them was a Committee on Special Education (CSE) Chairperson — nor did I know what that meant. All I knew was that my mom had a meeting with them every year—although I didn't know until much later in life what it was, and how it affected me.

Throughout my elementary school years, I would gravitate toward adults more than I would toward my peers because I liked to talk to them more. I related to adults because I have been talking to them since I could talk; doctors, nurses and therapists all discussed my disability with me.

Every day after lunch, we had twenty minutes outside on the playground at our elementary school. When I wasn't talking to the Noon-Hour Aides, I was taking a nap in the tunnel that was on the playground because of how taxing my physical disability was on my body.

Inside its walls, my elementary school had two floors, but it did not have an elevator, so I had to walk up two flights of stairs to get up to the class and then down the two flights to get down to my next class of the day, on the first floor.

In my first-grade year, I had a majority, if not all, of my subjects within one classroom, except for Music, which was on the second floor of the building. It wasn't until about fourth grade in which I had to go upstairs to the second floor for two subjects: Math and Music.

For safety reasons, since I required assistance to transition from the first to the second floor of the building, I needed to leave class early so I wasn't on the stairs at the same time as the other students. I know that this was to keep me safe but it also kept me apart from all of the kids.

Although Music was upstairs on the second floor, and it was difficult and tiring for me to climb the stairs, I loved that class. I didn't have that great of a singing voice, but I still sang because I liked to. When I was younger, I didn't care that I didn't have the voice of a great singer. I sang because it was fun and it made me feel good.

For physical education, I was in a general class, but I had an adaptive physical education teacher who, at times, gave me different tasks than the other students because I was physically incapable of doing what they were doing. An example of this is when the Fitnessgram™ Pacer Test came around, the other students ran from one side of the gymnasium to the other, where I only ran a quarter of that distance.

Up until I was about seven or eight years old, in second grade at Elsmere Elementary School, I had to have Botox injections in my legs and casts put onto them periodically so my muscles and heel cords would lengthen. This required an overnight stay at the hospital; coming in on a Sunday, leaving on a Monday.

One time, when I had the casts on my legs, it didn't feel right — I had these casts on my legs enough times where I knew what it was supposed to feel like, and this just wasn't it. Of course, this happened on a weekend (what luck!), so our choices were either the emergency room, waiting until Monday and calling Shriners, or having my dad cut the right cast off with his saw. My dad ended up cutting it off because of how much pain I was in. When the cast finally came off, we could see why I was in so much pain: The fiberglass was cutting into the top of my foot.

We called Shriners the following Monday, and I went back in and had a new cast put on.

When I was finally old enough, I was scheduled for a surgery to lengthen my heel cords and do a few other things to my legs. The whole surgery lasted five hours.

Coming out of it, I was a loon—the nurses got a kick out of it because I spoke "Pig Latin"!

In my second-grade year, the doctors and my parents discussed that the Botox injections were becoming less and less effective, so it was time for me to undergo a surgery on my legs. Because my muscles were tight, the purpose of this surgery was to "snip" them and put them in casts, which stretched them; so, after the surgery, they put me in casts from my hips to my toes. They were made in such a way as to where my knee was bent just enough to where it wasn't uncomfortably straight all the time that I was in the casts. I remember being out of school for two weeks, and my teacher and aide came to my house to visit me one day.

Because I was out of school for about six to eight weeks while I recovered from the operation, I had a tutor come in a few days a week to make sure that I kept up with my studies until I was ready to go back to school. I was happy with that because the tutor was my one-on-one aide, so I got to visit with her a few times a week while she helped me keep up with my studies.

In my third-grade year, we were given orange booklets that were meant to help us write cursive. I thoroughly enjoyed that and—to this day—my handwriting is a mixture of both cursive and print writing. It's sad that schools do not teach students how to write cursive anymore. Actually, come to think of it, I think that my class was one of the last to learn cursive in school.

I remember another time during that particular school year, I was eating a clementine during snack time and choked on it. Because of that experience, I was afraid to eat them again and I didn't pick up another until about five years later.

In my fourth-grade year, I remember one time in math class when I wasn't getting this one times table correct (seven times six), I told my teacher that I would write it one million times and hand it to her. 2017 marks eleven years since I told her I would do that, and I'm *still* working on completing it. I didn't realize back then how tall an order it was to write seven times six over and over again until my goal of one million times was reached.

Music was instruction in the classroom only up until fourth-grade. During that year, I joined the school's choir, which was a combination of fourth and fifth-grade students. My sister was in choir with me, and although she is shorter than me while standing, she would be taller than me when we sang because she had to go up on the risers, and I would have to sit in a chair in the front row of the risers. Nine times out of ten, it was pretty much just me in the front row, so it got pretty lonely.

. . . .

People have a fear of *metaphorically* falling, but I had a fear of *literally* falling. At one point in my elementary school career, I fell so much (and sometimes said I fell when I didn't, or made a bigger deal of the fall than there should have been just so I could get out of things that I didn't want to do—like schoolwork) that my mother told the school that I was to call home when I actually fell and the person who answered the phone—most often my father—would ask me questions like; "Did you hit your head?" That was the biggest question for me growing up because I have a shunt, which is the mechanism in my head that drains the cerebral fluid from my brain, down a tube, where it is then absorbed into my stomach.

I was born at twenty-five weeks. I was born in November when I should have been born in February. With that came some difficulties. For example, I had a Grade-Four brain bleed within a week of being born, which is what prompted the need for the shunt to be put into my head. The doctors told my family that, like any other piece of technology, this shunt *will* fail. It's just a matter of *when* it will fail.

And it did just that about ten years later in my fourth-grade year. I was in Newport, Rhode Island, on April vacation, and at about 5:30 in the morning, I went into my parents' room in our hotel room and told my mother that I had a headache. Thinking that it was just a headache and nothing more, she gave me Tylenol and told me to get in bed with her and sleep, in case I needed something else during the night.

A few hours later, I started vomiting. The vomiting brought with it *horrendous* pain. The pain was as if my brain was getting too big for my skull, as if it would break my skull open at any moment. This pain happened every time that I vomited because of the pressure that was building up in my head.

At 10:30 in the morning, my father said that we should probably call my pediatrician, so we did. We then went to the Emergency Room in Newport where they took a CAT scan and said I was in shunt failure. Following that, we were informed that we had two options: We could go home by helicopter or by ambulance to Hasbro Children's Hospital in Providence. My parents decided to go to Hasbro since I had a new neurosurgeon at home whom we had not even seen yet. My mom and I took an ambulance to the hospital and my dad was in our car behind us. The next day, I had emergency surgery to have the shunt replaced. I don't remember much after that in terms of that particular surgery.

After my surgery, I was so "down in the dumps" because I was self-conscious about my head—about my scar. So I got special permission from the school's principal to wear a hat to school (because there is a rule in all of the schools within the district that no hats were allowed to be worn in school).

So, when it was finally time for me to go back to school, I was greeted by everyone in the cafeteria wearing hats—so I didn't feel like the Lone Ranger! It brought a huge smile to my face; I was so happy to see that my school supported me!

About seven months later, in the fall of fourth grade, I started getting persistent headaches, which was a sign of the shunt failing. My parents again dragged me back to the doctors where another CAT scan was performed. The doctor told us that the shunt was failing and he needed to replace it. I told him that I was unable to have it replaced now because I was scheduled to go up to Double H Ranch® ski instructor dinner to talk about the ski program. It was important for me to do this because it was my way of giving back to the ranch. The doctor reluctantly agreed to schedule my surgery for the following week and said that if my symptoms got worse between now and then to give him a call.

A short time after I got back to school, I was sitting in the hall taking off my boots and I just broke down. My teacher asked me what was wrong and I told her that I didn't like that I was different. I didn't like having the shunt; I didn't like having to go through the surgeries. She said, matter of factly, that if I didn't have the shunt, if I didn't go through the surgeries when they failed, I would not be here. She was right. That conversation changed my outlook on my shunt and the surgeries; although I still didn't like going through them, I understood that it was a necessary part of my life; it was what was keeping me alive.

Another time, I was talking to my doctor about my scars (everywhere on my body: my head, stomach, hips, thighs, legs, and calves) and how I told him that I didn't like them, or removing my shirt, or wearing shorts, and he told me that my scars were "battle scars," and I should show them proudly, as each one was a battle that I won (I knew what he meant, but I still don't like going shirtless or wearing shorts, to this day).

. . . .

One of the many highlights of my fifth-grade year was writing a business letter to a providence in Canada. I was given New Brunswick. Looking back on this experience, I remember that some students did not receive anything back from their letters, but I did. I was elated because I was excited to learn more about them.

Another highlight of my fifth-grade year was in the fall of that year when I went to Becket, Massachusetts for five days with the entire fifth-grade from my elementary school as well as fifth-graders from other schools, to what they call "Nature's Classroom," where our classroom is nature. Because it would be hard for me to do basic things—such as shower—my father went with me and stayed with me for the duration of the trip.

One night while we were there, we simulated the Underground Railroad. Because of my physical disability, I did not participate like everyone else did. I was already at the Safe House when they got there; sweeping the floor while everyone was out attempting to get to it.

Like I said earlier, my father came with me to Nature's Classroom. He was with us in the Safe House and sat in the corner while we talked out what we were going to do when the other students came and how we were going to manage it all.

Even though I wasn't able to experience all of the Underground Railroad, I was happy that I could participate in a small way.

Later that same year, another project that we were to do was on sea animals, and I was given the Narwhal whale. We had to create a PowerPoint presentation with sound effects and transitions to be played for our parents a few weeks later. This was the beginning of my fascination with technology.

Cub Scouts and Boy Scouts

My mother was always the protective parent, and she also said, "If you don't want to do something, you don't have to." My father was the other end of that spectrum, "If you start something, you finish it."

Here's one example: When I was in elementary school, I started in Cub Scouts in my local Pack—which met at the American Legion Post down the street from me. I loved it because I was able to get out and socialize with people. I was able to make more friends. Cub Scouts was also a way for my father and me to have father/son bonding time because we would go on camping trips on our own—leaving my mother and sister home alone for a weekend (such as at the Boy Scout Jamboree in Fort Ticonderoga, New York) or Rotary Scout Reservation (located in Averill Park, New York,[1]) where I stayed for four days as a Cub Scout, but I stayed for about ten days when I went into Boy Scouts.

I went through Cub Scouts and received the Arrow of Light, which was the final badge that was awarded in Cub Scouts—it was also the only badge from Cub Scouts that I could wear on my Boy Scout uniform.

I stayed in Scouting until I achieved the rank of First Class, which is the fourth rank up to Eagle Scout: Scout, Tenderfoot, Second Class, **First Class**, Star, Life, Eagle.[2] After earning First Class, I only had three levels left to earn in order to become an Eagle Scout.

Around the time that I earned the First Class rank, the then-Scoutmaster stepped down and another stepped up in his place. I was sad about the previous Scoutmaster stepping down because the first Scoutmaster would include me in activities that the Troop did and help me any way he could, but when the new one came in, it was as if I didn't exist.

So, one night, my father told me that it was time to get ready to go to the meeting, and I told him that I didn't want to go. He had asked me my reasoning as to why I didn't want to go, and I told him that it was because I didn't feel included in Scouting anymore, because of how I felt the new Scoutmaster was treating me.

He reminded me that it was my choice to leave, but he supported my decision nonetheless. Over the years, though, I have regretted leaving because the rank of Eagle looks good on a resume (which is partially why I was doing it in the first place, next to the bonding of the Scouts). Even though I left a few years ago, I still catch myself wondering, "What would it be like if I had stuck with it and achieved the Eagle rank? Where would I be today?"

A few years later, I was in my Biology class and had a friend in it from my Boy Scout troop. He told me that his father had taken over the bookkeeping of the troop and that he still had my paperwork, if I ever wanted to go back into Scouting—which they both wanted me to do. I cannot say that I didn't think about it, but I weighed the options because the replacement Scoutmaster who didn't include me in anything was still in that position, so I felt as if I would be back where I was when I stopped Scouting.

· · · · · · · · · ·

In elementary school, I was one of the lucky students to have one one-on-one aide throughout my whole time in elementary school. Karen Anthony was my aide and she was a great influence on me. I will always be grateful for her pushing me to do my best, but for also being sensitive enough to know when I was at my limit.

FORGING THROUGH
THE ELEMENTARY YEARS

by Karen Anthony

We all called him the mayor of Slingerlands Elementary. I had never seen a five-year-old with the spirit or personality of a sixty-year-old man and I was the lucky one who was assigned to him.

Lou the kindergartener was larger than life with his personality. His personality, not his physical handicap, was the first thing you saw. His gift of gab was incredible. Lou used this gift to engage with the adults in his world. It was also his tool to help him with schoolwork avoidance. He truly thought he was winning but we all knew his number and made sure the job got done.

First grade proved to have many challenges for Lou. We were in a different elementary school with two floors. The downside was that this was an old school with *no elevator*! Lou and I would stand at the bottom of the staircase and look up before we started. It was as if we were looking up at Mt. Everest. Of course, my biggest challenge was to keep him focused on the stair climbing instead of talking and asking me questions. Yes, there were slips. But I always caught him.

I believe second grade was a huge transition year for Lou. His transportation to and from school was on a small handicap bus. I was worried that he was missing out on socialization with his peers since he was the only student on the bus. I knew that he would be able to get up and down the bus steps with adult help. One of my goals for Lou was to be just like the other kids. I brought my idea to his physical therapist. She was totally on board with my idea. So after a few weeks of training and practice, Lou overcame another hurdle. He was now riding the "*big*" bus with his peers. Of course, he chose to sit up front so he could have great conversations with his bus driver and bus aide instead of his peers.

Field trips always proved to be a challenge for both of us. I was always thinking, "How would I be able to make sure Lou could enjoy this field trip, but at the same time, also keep him safe?" Planning was key to our successful day! I was also blessed to have a wonderful staff for support at all times.

Fifth grade proved to be such a fabulous year. Lou and I were like a well-oiled machine. We knew each other like the back of our hands. He knew when I would push him to do his very best and he knew that he had to do his very best. I knew when he was doing his personal best and when he had reached his limit. It was rare for Lou to be upset or to not try his best. He always wanted to please everyone.

Nature's Classroom was the highlight of fifth grade. It was four days away, at a YMCA camp in Becket, MA. Adaptations were made for Lou and his group so that he could participate and also be successful. My proudest moment was when we took the night hike up a steep incline in the pitch dark. We needed to get to an area to do some nighttime experiments. We managed to do it with a lot of perseverance and physical force. I couldn't have been more proud of Lou and myself for accomplishing this activity.

Fifth grade graduation day was approaching. Lou and I had a sweet conversation about moving on.

He wanted me to move onto the middle school with him. I told him that I had done my job to prepare him for life at the middle school and that he could hold his head up high. I assured him that I was confident that he was ready (even though he felt he wasn't). I told him that he needed to trust me. Just be yourself and hold your head up high. "Do your personal best," I told him. "You will do fine, I'm *positive*," I insisted. On graduation day, I wept with pride and joy as Lou walked across the stage to receive his diploma. I couldn't have been prouder if he had been my own child.

My main goal over the course of six years was to prepare Lou for middle school life. As a special education aide, you always want your student to make improvements and to be as independent as possible. I had always worked with students with just academic needs. I had never worked with a student with academic and physical handicap needs. It was just as challenging for me as it was for Lou. We learned to overcome obstacles and to strengthen our abilities to endure our day. I definitely feel like I made a difference in Lou's life. Determination was the keyword for both Lou and me. If Lou could find a way to move through his life then I could also. Our school district should have more kids like Lou. His love of life, people, and conversation is truly a gift.

MY MIDDLE SCHOOL YEARS

In the fall of 2008, I went from elementary school to middle school. The summer before my first year of middle school, I went around with my mom and sister to see where my classes were, where my locker was, etc., to get the lay of the land.

In middle school, I participated in the annual planning for my IEP for the first time. I was becoming more independent in most things. For one, I no longer had a one-on-one aide all day long, but just for going from classroom to classroom as hallways can be a dangerous place for someone with balance issues. I would also try to resolve anything concerning my accommodations by myself, but for the things that I could not, I brought in my "secret weapon": my mother. And she would *not* take "no" for an answer — which was great for me, but not so great for my school!

An example of this was when I had to take music class. One year, I was put into a class that was down in the basement of the school, which would have been fine, if there was a way for one of the school's elevators to get down to the basement, but there was not. So, the only way for me to get down to the basement to the classroom was to go down the stairs. I knew that was not in line with what my accommodations were supposed to be.

I talked to my physical therapist about this, and she brought me to the stairwell to observe how I would do walking down it. After I walked down and back up with her, she said that I could go down the stairs. She was actually wondering why I shouldn't have to do it. Yes, I *could* do it, but that didn't mean that I *should* have to do it. I tried talking to her about it, but she wouldn't listen to me.

When my mother got home from work that night, I talked to her about this, and she agreed with me. She said that the elevators in the school and the ramp in the front of the school were there for kids like me. That there was only one place in that whole school that was not accessible, so why did they have to schedule me into that one classroom? She told me to speak to the vice principal since he was in charge of scheduling. So I did. He said he would look into it. He talked to my physical therapist and she said I was capable of climbing the stairs so she saw no reason why my classroom needed to be changed. So he would not change my schedule. I was frustrated that they would not listen to me, but they would be sorry. It was time for my secret weapon to become involved.

I told him that my mother wanted to speak to him about it. He called my mom to talk to her about it. He told her that I was capable of climbing stairs and there was not another class that he could put me into. My mom did not like that and she lit into him, telling him that she was aware of what I was capable of, that was not the issue. The issue was that I should not have to and that the school was obligated to make accommodations for me. He said that we would have to have a meeting with the CSE chairperson, that there was nothing he could do. My mom told him that was fine, to just let her know when the meeting was. The next day, he called me into his office and my schedule had been changed. He moved me into a music class that was on the second floor of the school, which the elevator *could* get to. Needless to say, my physical therapist wasn't happy about it.

I learned an important lesson here: That the adults in the school might not necessarily understand my accommodations and that I could make a difference.

Another time, when I was in middle school, for Physical Education I had what my district referred to as the "swimming unit", which was supposed to be in the winter months when it was too cold to go outside (thank gosh the pool was heated!). The challenge there was the time that it took me to get changed from my clothes into my bathing suit, and then from my wet bathing suit back into my clothes (which was always a challenge!).

One year (my sixth-grade year), I had Physical Education as my second class of the day and Earth Science as my third. Because it took me so long to change from my bathing suit back into my clothes, I was almost always late to my Earth Science class. The first few times, my teacher understood, but as it started happening more and more, that's when she became concerned.

So, I was put into a fitness class for the time that the rest of my class was in the swimming unit. With that, there was no changing in and out of swimsuits, so I wasn't late to my Earth Science class — my teacher was happy about that!

So, that's what we did for the following two years: every swimming unit, I was moved out of my class into whatever class was in the fitness center during the period in which I had physical education. I got to meet a lot of wonderful teachers that way.

. . . .

In my sixth-grade year, I had Resource Room, which helped with organization as well as reinforcing any concepts learned in class that were not very well understood by the students within the room.

Because of this, I could not take a language. At the time, taking a language was a requirement for graduation with a New York State Regents Diploma, unless you were exempt from it. I was adamant, though, that I wanted to take a language, so I talked to my mom, who in turn talked to the school about it, and I was put into a language the following school year.

In my seventh-grade year, I took my first year of Spanish. I have always loved the language, and was sad that I couldn't take it the year before because of having Resource Room in my schedule.

I also remember in my Science class that year, we had "Life Science." We dissected a worm. My whole class was so grossed out at the idea that my teacher did the dissection himself and showed us what was what in terms of the worm. It was amazing to see how small all of its organs were!

That year, my class also took a trip to the Bronx Zoo. At that time, a class could only go on a field trip if there was some sort of educational reason for doing so. To make this an educational trip, my teacher and the teachers for the other Life Science classes, got together and created a packet that we had to fill out while we were exploring the zoo.

In my eighth-grade year, I took my second, and final, year of Spanish within the middle school. This year was particularly important because we were gearing up for the New York State Language Proficiency Exams, which were the equivalent of Regents Exams in classes such as U.S. History (that I took in my eleventh-grade year) and English Language Arts (which I also took in my eleventh-grade year.) This test consisted of a listening portion as well as reading comprehension and multiple-choice questions.

This test counted for one language credit in high school if I passed the exam, so I was rather nervous about it, although I was well prepared for it.

When I received that exam back, I looked it over and realized that I earned a 91% on the test with only two years (seventh and eighth-grade) of Spanish under my belt. I was really happy about that, but at the same time, like my English and U.S. History Regents, I was wondering what I got wrong on the exam. Sometimes I *still* wonder what I could have gotten wrong on the exam, but that's just me: I strive for perfection and, if I don't achieve it, I wonder what I did wrong, and sometimes, I obsess over it—that is a trait that has carried with me throughout my schooling, from elementary school to college.

Although I had wonderful experiences in middle school, I didn't leave the school without having at least one huge hurdle to overcome.

The shunt that I had placed in my head in fourth grade failed, although we don't know exactly how. I started displaying symptoms of shunt failure after getting hit in the head with a shoe in dance class in physical education. My mom asked my guidance counselor to get information from all of my teachers about any changes in my performance or any noticeable neurological differences (such as balance, concentration, or memory issues). The teachers did come back with some concerns and with this, along with the knowledge of the shoe to my head, my parents thought that it was a good idea to schedule an appointment with my neurosurgeon.

At the appointment, a CAT scan was performed and it showed that fluid had built up in my head. That was when the doctor used the dreaded "S" word again: surgery. When I heard that, I immediately cried into my mother's chest. I begged the doctor not to make me have the surgery, and he agreed. He told me that if anything happens, to call him and he will schedule the surgery.

I went back to school trying to ignore what the doctor had told me because it was too upsetting to think about.

I was in Science class, and I started to get dizzy, which happened for about three days straight. Every time that this happened, I went to visit the nurse in the health office. After the third time of this happening, on a Friday, I called my father. Through tears, I told him that I think I should get the surgery. He called my neurosurgeon and scheduled the surgery for that coming Monday.

At the end of my eighth-grade year, our middle school had a "Moving Up Ceremony" for the eighth-graders who were going to be incoming ninth-graders. The Moving Up Ceremony was in one of the gymnasiums of the high school.

While at the Moving Up Ceremony, I received an award for the high grade that I had earned on the Spanish Proficiency Exam that I had taken earlier that year. It was an honor to receive it and to be recognized for my hard work in language.

. . . .

I had several aides throughout my time in the middle school, and one has written a piece for this book, but since he was my aide in the middle school and high school, I have included it following the next chapter.

My High School Years

In the fall of 2011, I transitioned from middle school to high school.

Going into high school, I continued that bout of independence. Like in middle school, if I had a problem, I would do everything in my power to rectify it, but if I couldn't get anywhere, I would bring in my mother. Thankfully, for the school, I didn't have to bring her in often, but when I did, they weren't happy because she would talk to the Committee on Special Education (CSE) Chairperson more often than not because I was finally in the school where the office was located (which was good for me as well, so I could go and talk to them myself if I needed to).

LOUIS A. VENDETTI

My Freshman Year of High School

My freshman year of high school was bad academically. When I went from middle to high school, I didn't really care about work. There was this one paper that I wrote in English that I had trouble writing because my computer malfunctioned. I kept making excuses, and eventually, it came to where my teacher was going to write me up for not having the assignment in to him, but my aide at the time talked him out of it.

Although, there was this one time in my physical education class where I *was* written up, I didn't have to serve that write-up. I was written up for not coming to class, even though I had a reason that I wasn't in class — I didn't ever skip class.

In my freshman year of high school, I was in a ninth-grade PE class which was a "general" PE class. Once, we did basketball, and my mom didn't want me to be in the same room with basketballs because she was afraid that I would get hit in the back of the head with one.

My Sophomore Year of High School

In the tail end of my freshman year at my high school, I saw a poster on the wall advertising that the district's technology department was looking for students to help them in a new initiative that they were going to start up called the "Student Help Desk." The students who manage this desk are qualified students who are able to go out and complete tickets and/or other tasks like the district's technology, but on a smaller scale. The district's technology department is responsible for the entire district, but the Student Help Desk is only responsible for the high school.

While I was working with the technology department, I was given tickets that some teachers sent in. Once, I was assigned a ticket from my Global History teacher in tenth grade. She had put in a ticket for her Promethean board not functioning correctly. So, I went down there with another person from the Student Help Desk to see if we could fix the problem. When we got there, the teacher explained her problem to us and we went to work. We found the problem—which was actually a faulty lightbulb, nothing to do with the Promethean board itself. Because we didn't have a new lightbulb with us at the time, we told her that we would report it to the tech department and someone from there would be back either later that day or the following day.

We had tickets like that just about every day. The ones that the technology department thought that we could handle, we were given. It was a great experience to learn how to fix the various pieces of technology that we were exposed to in the high school.

Around the same time that I found out about the Student Help Desk opportunity, I took a tour of a technical school that my district had a relationship with. I took a liking to the web design course that they have there, called Internet Applications, because I wanted to create an iPhone application when I was younger. At the time, though, I didn't realize that that particular course had a "prerequisite" called "Gaming", although it had nothing to do with the course. One was to design games, and the other was to design websites and smartphone applications. I thought to myself, "How could the one be related to the other?" I quickly found out that they are not, that there was no correlation between the two whatsoever, other than the fact that they were taught by the same teacher.

After I toured the school, I had a decision to make: whether I was going to take that course or not. Ultimately, I decided to do so, that meant that I went to the technical school for half of the day and spent the other half of the day in our high school. Because I was going to the technical school, I was unable to take a language, and my father was upset about this because he knew how much I like Spanish. He told me that I would regret not taking Spanish in my last two years of high school — and I do, but don't tell my dad.

My Junior Year of High School

Going into my junior year, I was trying to psych myself up for the gaming course. Although I had convinced myself in the beginning that I wouldn't like it — I ended up loving it. I was able to use Photoshop CS6, which was great because I could create images with it — I actually created a get-well card for my dad with it.

At the end of learning Photoshop, though, we had to take a test to obtain a certification. That was considered an exam for the class, and we had to pass it in order to pass the class itself. Thankfully, we were able to take the test multiple times until we passed because it took me four times to pass the exam.

What frustrated me about the test was that we had to wait five days from one attempt to another, and when we went to take it again, the test was entirely different then when we took it the time before—so there really wasn't any proper way to prepare for the exam. We also had a combination of multiple choice and practical, hands-on questions. The hands-on questions required us to complete the task the way that the test wanted us to—even if we knew another way to complete that task, which frustrated many of my classmates, as well as myself.

In order to pass the exam, you had to earn a score of seven hundred out of a thousand points—a thousand being a perfect score.

- The first time that I took the exam, I got in the high three-hundreds: 366

- Before taking the actual Photoshop exam a second time, I took the practice test for Adobe Photoshop CS6 and received a score of three hundred.

- The second time, it was 463.

- The third time, it was 561.

- The fourth, and final time that I took the exam, I received a passing score of 732.

At the end of my junior year, I also had two Regents Exams to take: English Language Arts and U.S. History.

I remember the grade on my English Language Arts grade exam because it was so low. Usually, I would get high grades on anything that I submitted for a grade in an English class, but for some reason, the state graded the way that they did, and I received a 73%. My U.S. History Regents Exam was a lot nicer at 89%. The only problem that I had with this grade is the fact that I didn't get up into the nineties. It amazes me that I could earn such a high grade on something that I thought was challenging (because I had to memorize dates and such), and earn such a low grade on something that I'm proficient in. It makes no sense.

My Senior Year of High School

In my senior year of high school, I had a lot of things to do to get ready for graduation, but I also had to get ready for college. Luckily for me, Hudson Valley had an Instant Admit Day at my high school where I could just bring my high school transcript and be accepted on the spot.

In the summer before my senior year of high school, I received the answer to my unspoken prayer: A letter informing me that I was recommended by my teacher at the trade school to take a College in the High School class called "Introduction to Entrepreneurship." Since I was going to Hudson Valley anyway, although at the time I was going to be going down the Computer Information Systems track, I thought that this would be a great way for me to get my foot in the door and for me to see how a college course actually worked. This course was in the fall of 2014.

I was beyond elated to start this program; I couldn't wait until the school year began. When I went into the trade school on the first day, I was told that the course would start the following week and I was to report to that class for the duration of the time that I was supposed to attend my regular trade school class—that because I was taking the College in the High School course, I didn't have to be in the course I was originally enrolled in, at least for the first sixteen weeks.

This class was filled with the "best of the best" from the various classes of that trade school. They were from just about all of the different areas of study throughout the campus.

Back when I took the course, our textbook was *Who Owns the Ice House* by Gary G. Schoeniger and Clifton L. Taulbert. It chronicles the lessons that Taulbert learns from his Uncle Cleve.[3] The book was supplemented by videos on a companion website that we had to watch before the next time our class met. Most students didn't like the videos because they thought they were "dry" or "boring." They didn't really feel that they held any value, although within the videos were different golden nuggets given by entrepreneurs like Brian Scudamore who is the chief executive officer of 1-800-Got-Junk?®. The videos talked about the challenges that each entrepreneur faced and how they overcome them. I found them valuable, indispensable at times, although I did see what my classmates were saying when they thought they were dry and boring.

For the final project of the course, we had to do a condensed marketing plan for a business that we wanted to create. So, my group created "No Fear Fitness." I was paired with two other people, although that pairing didn't stay true until the end since the person whom we were paired with didn't do his part and the group members for another group left, so the person left behind was paired up with us.

We found out after our final projects were assigned, that some of the students had dropped out due to their class commitments. In one of the classes, the students had to have one thousand hours of doing hair and makeup (Cosmetology), so they elected to drop the course and go back to their classes so they wouldn't fall behind.

There were two people from the Cosmetology program in one group, so that left the person not enrolled in that program in the class by herself, having to create the marketing plan all on her own. Our professor didn't like that idea, so she thought that she would pair us together.

At the end of the semester, my professor said that she was recommending me to take the next course in the sequence of entrepreneurship courses: Entrepreneurial Process (ENTR 120). I emailed the department chair at the time and inquired about this. I asked if there were any discounts for this class, like there were for Introduction to Entrepreneurship, and he said that there were not, that the full tuition had to be paid for the course.

With this in mind, after *a lot* of thinking, I chose to just wait and take that course once I was a matriculated student at the college.

. . . .

The fall 2014 semester ended in December of that year, so still being in high school, I had about four months left until the end of school year, so I had to go back into my regularly scheduled class at the technical school.

While there, one of the things that we had to prepare for was another certification exam. The exam was much like the one that I took in my previous year, but just on a different topic. This time, it was on Adobe InDesign CS6.

This exam was structured the same as the Photoshop CS6 exam: I had to get at least seven hundred out of a thousand to pass the exam and it was a combination of multiple choice and practical, hands-on type questions.

- The first time that I took the exam, I got in the low four-hundreds: 425.

- The second time, it was 475.

- The third time, it was the same as the second: 475.

- The fourth time that I took the exam I earned a 575.

- The fifth, and final, time that I took the exam, I earned a passing score of seven hundred.

. . . .

On October 28, 2014, Instant Admit Day happened in the counseling center of my high school, and I was accepted on the spot. The Admissions counselor even said that because I came to the Instant Admit Day, and because my grades were stellar, that he was going to waive the college-placement tests for me, which was a relief because I don't like taking exams.

When I was back at my high school, though, Physical Education was one of the best classes that I took that year that left a lasting impact on me. That was because, like my sophomore and junior years, I could pick what I did for twenty weeks from a predetermined list, and that's the same for the spring as well. The teacher that I had for this particular round, though, took me out of my comfort zone and helped me actually participate. In Ballroom Dance, for example, I didn't dance with anyone; I just danced with myself on the sidelines of the gymnasium. One of my proudest moments of that unit was that I was able to dance to the beat of the music.

My aide and I were rather surprised that I was able to dance to the beat, considering I was dancing with my crutches on a mat and trying not to slip off of it or trip over it. I was so over the moon that I wanted to show my teacher. When I did, she was very impressed, which made my confidence in my dancing skyrocket. I continued to impress her, which made me proud of myself.

In the spring of my senior year, I received a letter from my elementary school inviting me back for their senior assembly in May. In that assembly, we were recognized and commended for our hard work throughout the years in our district and our future plans were talked about.

One of the fun things that happened during the assembly was when our fifth-grade photos were shown on a PowerPoint presentation as our names were called to go to the front of the auditorium. My fifth-grade photo does *not* look anything like how I look now. I was more "chubby" back then, where in my senior year, I was more "thinned out."

. . . .

In middle school, I had a few aides throughout my time there. I had one for a long while, though: Paul Moylan. I first met him back in 2008, when I transitioned from my elementary school to the middle school. He was a kind man who helped make my transition a smooth one.

I was lucky to be able to have Paul Moylan as my aide in high school, too. He was able to see how much I'd grown from middle school, and witness some of my *hugest* accomplishments throughout my time with him in the high school.

Because he was my aide in both middle school and high school, I have put Paul Moylan's testimony following this chapter.

My Travels with Lou

by Paul Moylan

In 2008, I first met Louis Vendetti as a new sixth-grade student at Bethlehem Middle School. I knew that name since I had gone to school with his Uncle John, and I knew who his father was from being just a couple of years older. What I didn't realize, at the time, was that this was a bit of a "package deal!" Lou had a twin sister named Loren, who was also going to be a fairly constant presence over the school years to come!

What I remember most about the middle school year I worked with Lou was his dogged determination to ask three thousand questions of his teachers, where one or two would have been sufficient! He wanted not just the answers to questions but the root causes of *why* they were the answers! This was a great trait for a young student and Lou could also keep up a conversation with an adult far better than any sixth grader I had ever known! He definitely had "the gift of gab" and most of his teachers appreciated that quality.

He was a very conscientious student and used his time wisely to get his work done in class. Mobility was more the issue we had to work around. But it never was a real barrier for Lou. Whether using his trusty crutches (which he totally outgrew by the time he got to high school!) or his walker (which he *really* outgrew by high school), Lou operated them with great skill and efficiency. He "outran" me on several occasions in the hallways!

Physical Education class was also very interesting as Lou would participate in all the activities he could. And some of those activities, like swimming, he participated in with great zeal! I think my favorite time was his complete devotion to the line dance song, "Cotton Eyed Joe." I swear, at any time, he was going to bust right out of those crutches and completely "bust a move!" Great attitude and great enthusiasm. It was a very good year of working with a fine young man!

MY TRAVELS WITH LOU PART II
by Mr. Moylan

I worked with Lou a little bit during his seventh-grade year, and then I transferred up to Bethlehem High School. I reconnected with him when he entered his junior year. My job was to assist him with transitions from class to class and to accompany him to the Capital Region Center for Technical Education (B.O.C.E.S.). Lou was interested in computers and in learning software utilization and development.

Basically, Lou taught himself most of the next two years at B.O.C.E.S. To say the instruction he received was not exactly "up to par" would be an understatement! But, with that level of challenge facing him, he worked that much harder to learn! With additional support from the teaching assistant who was in the classroom for both of the years there, he continued to gain confidence and was selected for the National Technical Honor Society his senior year.

Meanwhile, back at the high school, I continued to go to Physical Education with Lou. He enjoyed archery (and was quite good!), bowling, yoga (modified just for him) and most of all, ballroom dancing! Lou, in consort with the PE teacher, was able to learn dance steps while using his crutches! This was quite a sight to see and he relished not having to sit on the sidelines for this activity! He even made of a video of those dance steps!

Lou was active outside of class, as well. His main responsibility was the lead organizer of the annual "Hat Day" to raise money for the "The Double H Camp." His spirit over the years carried that fundraiser to record amounts as students were allowed to wear hats at school for the donation of $1.00 to the camp fund.

MY TRAVELS WITH LOU, PART II cont. by Mr. Moylan

Summarizing my three years of working with Lou in school is easy! It was a great pleasure to know someone so mature for their age and watch them grow even more over that time. When Lou was a senior at B.O.C.E.S. he got his first taste of a college business course, with college credit attached! He excelled in it and his future direction began to take shape. The foundation that he had laid, prior to that, was already well established! I am just glad I got to be a small part of it as the journey continues!

THE MONTHS AND DAYS
LEADING UP TO COLLEGE

The months before my first semester were busy ones. I had to get advised for my classes at the college, I had to go to the Center for Access and Assistive Technology to make sure that I received the college accommodations that I am entitled to. I had to make sure that my email was working. I had to make sure that I could log into Blackboard (because I had an online class my first semester: Computer Concepts and Applications I—CMPT 101).

April 21, 2015 was my round of new student orientation. I learned about the college, but I also received my classes that day, too. Before all of this, though, we went on a tour of the campus with the tour guides.

I remember the day being very, very hectic. There were a lot of students at that orientation, but there were only a few advisors. We were all seated at round tables, and sometimes it was hard to hear the presenter, as I don't remember her using a microphone of any sort, just her own voice to project.

Although I listened to the presentations that were going on, and how to navigate the various portals that the college uses, when it came down to the time of actually registering for our classes, I needed *a lot* of help. For some people, the process took only a few minutes, but for me, it took about an hour. Needless to say, I didn't feel very confident in my ability to navigate the system on my own—although that's nine times out of ten what I did for my classes. The first few times, I had help, but as the semesters went on, I felt more and more confident in how to use the system—and now I go in and check to see the enrollment of courses I already took (such as International and Intercultural Business—BADM 280) to see what the enrollment is like, just to keep my skills sharp. I don't want to lose the ability or knowledge to navigate the system.

After I was finished with setting up my schedule, I was upset with myself because I had signed up for classes every day of the week, Monday through Friday. I did not want to do that because I had been going to school Monday through Friday for the twelve years prior to that.

. . . .

About two months before the fall 2015 semester began, I put the start date of the semester into a countdown app on my phone so I would know how many days there were until the semester started. Doing that kind of heightened the anxiety that I felt, but at the same time, I was also excited because it was a new experience. I was excited for the new people that I would meet and the new experiences that I would have.

As the days drew closer to the start of the fall 2015 semester, I started to get nervous because, although I had been there the spring before, I would be navigating the campus on my own without an aide, like I had in the twelve years of school I had just come from.

PART II

. . . .

COLLEGE LIFE

THE FIRST SEMESTER

In my first semester (fall 2015), I had five classes: Computer Concepts and Applications I, English Composition I, College Forum, Intermediate Algebra, and General Psychology.

My first semester as a matriculated student was overwhelming to say the least. I remember going around with my schedule the first day not knowing where I was going. I was so nervous to meet my professors.

The then-Campus Chaplain asked me, "How are you?" And, hearing that soft, gentle voice utter those words, I immediately broke down crying because of how stressed I was—because of all of the unneeded stress that I had put onto myself.

He took me into his office and we proceeded to talk for a few minutes. Because of the nature of our conversation, he asked if I had seen anyone over in the Wellness Center. I told him that I had.

So, I set up weekly appointments with the Wellness Center, and went along with my first semester.

Computer Concepts and Applications I was my introduction into the Office 2013 Suite of Products: Word, PowerPoint, Excel, and Access.

I had used Word, PowerPoint, and Excel prior to taking this class, but I had never used it to the point of what most of the assignments required me to do. Prior to taking this course, I had never used Access, so it was kind of a learning curve for me, especially considering the steps and diagrams within the textbook were designed for a computer running Windows 8, and my computer was running Windows 7.

Needless to say, some of the assignments that we were assigned to do for the course were rather challenging, such as the introduction in the book itself—it was geared toward a computer with Windows 8 installed on it.

We had five modules within the course and then the final exam. The five modules were:

1. Office Fundamentals

2. Word

3. Excel

4. Access

5. PowerPoint

Office Fundamentals was going through all four of the products. We had basic things to do in each area. When we got into Word, though, that's when the course started to get challenging because we would dive deep into the different aspects of each program.

And our final exam was a few parts. We had to use all four programs to complete the final. We had to create pieces in different programs for vacation specials and upcoming tours that are going on during that particular vacation time. Creating the pieces of the final exam was kind of challenging because Microsoft Access and I do not necessarily get along that well—we didn't during class, we didn't during the final, and we do not to this day. I kind of have a love-hate relationship with it, but that's probably only because I didn't have enough time to play around with and learn the ins and outs of it to where I was comfortable with the program.

English Composition I was my first English course that I took at a college level. I had to do a research paper for the course (which was only worth twenty points, but it was weighted at about 25% of the course). This research paper was required by the department, so each English Comp I course had to do the same type of paper.

Toward the end of the semester, we had to do a five-minute presentation on where we were in our research papers, what we learned so far on our topic from our research, and where we are going with our research (as the paper wasn't due for a few weeks from the presentation). The presentation itself was us just "checking in" and telling our classmates about our research.

College Forum was a required course that all first-time, full-time (and part-time) students had to take in their first semester of enrollment to the college. It teaches you about the different resources on campus; the Public Safety Office with the Public Safety Officers and Peace Officers, among other things.

Sometime within my first semester, I heard of a rumor (of sorts) that if the professor didn't show up to class within fifteen minutes of it starting, that the students could leave and there was no class for that day.

However, that is not true. My College Forum professor put that rumor to rest. She gave us the following scenario:

Say that you have an exam the day that the professor is late. If you are not there because they were late, then you are unable to take the exam.

She went on to say that if you are not there to take the exam when it is administered, some professors do not allow for retakes, so you forfeited that exam.

Early on in the course, we also talked about the College's Statute of Limitation on Degree Completion, which states that the "requirements for degree completion are based on those stated in the catalog for the year a student matriculates in a specific program. A student will have a maximum of five (5) years from the date of matriculation to complete a degree based on those requirements. After the five (5) year limitation, requirements for all programs convert to those cited in the most current catalog. A student may opt for the current catalog requirements at any time."[4]

Intermediate Algebra was the first Math requirement for my degree. Prior to coming to college, I had taken this course three times. In my freshman year of high school, I was enrolled into it as it was a New York State Regents requirement to graduate with a high school diploma. In the second quarter of my freshman year, my math teacher put a comment on my report card that said, "Student is in danger of failing the course."

After learning this, I went to find out what my options were. I found out about a slower course that was called an "Excel Math" course. It split the curriculum into two years: the first half of the curriculum was covered in the first year, and the second half of the curriculum was covered in the second year. This was wonderful for many people because it allowed the teacher to spend more time on each of the units within the course content. It allowed for more room to learn each of the pieces of material.

After going into the Excel Intermediate Algebra course, I found that I understood the material easier than I did when I was in the regular course because we took more time to learn each of the different components. We didn't just fly through them like the regularly paced math class did.

After two years, I took the Math Regents Exam and received a grade in the seventies.

I knew going into the course that I was going to struggle with it, but as the course progressed through the semester, that thought just solidified more and more in my mind—to the point where I would think about withdrawing from it—and taking it the following semester—because I was right on the border of failing the course.

So, after talking it over with my family, and checking with the Financial Aid Office to make sure that it wouldn't negatively impact me if I withdrew, I went to the Business Advisement Center and filled out a withdrawal form, which I had to bring down to the registrar once it was completed.

As I was filling out the paper, a professor walked past me and saw that I was filling out the withdrawal form. We got talking, and he introduced himself as the Department Chair for Accounting, Entrepreneurship, and Marketing. Although I outwardly maintained my composure, I thought on the inside, *oh crud! I'm meeting my Department*

Chair while I'm filling out a withdrawal form for a class. What a nice first impression... not!

General Psychology was an overview of the different areas and thought patterns of Psychology. The professor that I took this course with made the course fun, although it was sometimes challenging to understand, but that was not his fault; Psychology is hard to learn within a sixteen-week time period.

Usually, I'm not good with exams, but I received good grades on at least one of his, which I was surprised about because, like I said, I am not a very good test-taker.

. . . .

This semester was a challenging one. At my advisement for the spring 2016 semester, I talked to my advisor about taking four classes instead of five. She allowed me to, but told me doing that would require me to take one more semester than I would have originally if I had taken five classes.

Starting in spring 2016, I lightened my course load and took four classes instead of five.

. . . .

Following this chapter, I have pieces from two of my friends: Wayne Sharp and Tanya Fredricks.

Wayne Sharp is a friend of mine that I met at my alma mater. He was my tutor for a few of my classes (Computer Concepts and Applications I, English Composition I, General Psychology, Intermediate Algebra, and Statistics).

I first met Wayne in the fall of 2015, when I was in my first round of Intermediate Algebra. At the time that I met him, I'd dug my hole so deep to where even he couldn't help me get out of it. So, I withdrew from Intermediate Algebra that semester, after realizing that I would not be able to recover from where I was in terms of my grade, so we both agreed to pick up fresh the next semester; spring 2016.

Tanya Fredricks is the clerk in the Center for Academic Engagement (CAE) at my alma mater. She is the first face that you see when you walk into the CAE, and she is always smiling. I remember back in the fall 2015 semester when I was nervous to move forward, and she talked to me for a few minutes, getting to know me and my situation. That was the start of a wonderful friendship that continues to this day.

THE VENDETTI SYNDROME

by Wayne Sharp

When I first met Lou, I saw a young man with no self-confidence. He was so unsure of himself that I had to take on the responsibility of being his tutor, mentor, and above all, his friend. I walked into this task thinking I was going to change his world and make him a man of confidence and strong will. Little did I know, Lou would teach me more about myself than I could ever have taught him about school.

Lou has a way to make even the most depressed and sad person smile and look at life in a whole new way. He taught me to look beyond my initial impression of a person and see what lies inside them. While tutoring him in MATH 110, Lou had the impression that he could not achieve a good grade. I wasn't sure if I was good enough to relay how to properly do the math. But with Lou's infectious laugh and positive attitude, he achieved his goal. Showing me that I can't judge a book by its cover, and to better understand where people come from and what they have lived through.

HVCC benefited greatly by having Lou as a student. Not only did he achieve greatness in his academic career, but he also brightened the day of every person he encountered. His smile, his kind words, and his willingness to listen to anyone's problems while offering an unbiased, and caring answer, or even just an ear to bend when you need to vent. The Vendetti Syndrome is the kindness and caring of your fellow man, even if life has given you a bad deal from the beginning. Lou may have to live his life in a wheelchair, but when he speaks, his words echo from the highest mountain, and his caring for others surpasses any disability he may have. I for one am very proud to consider him my friend, my life tutor, and my mentor.

The Sun Brings a New Day

by Tanya Fredricks

I have been asked to write a short entry on how Lou has affected me here at HVCC.

Where do I begin? I've been here in the CAE for three years. That is six semesters. I have known Lou for all of these. Though I don't remember exact details on our first meeting, I can tell you I am so glad that it happened. Lou is one of the sweetest, most kind-hearted souls I have ever met. He never has anything but a kind word for everyone and goes out of his way to be helpful and has a fantastic sense of humor.

What have I learned from Lou during his time here? Well, I have learned that there are some extraordinary people on this earth. Instead of letting his disability get him down, he embraces it and goes out of his way to push for people just like him. He is a proud member of a campground that caters to people with all kinds of disabilities and he absolutely shines when he is there. He even advocates for it. He has taught me to not let little things get me down because there are so many wonderful things still left in the world.

Have I grown as a person from having Lou in my life? I cannot stress how much. I could come into work, having the worst morning ever, and there he is, silly grin on his face, so happy to just be here. If anything, I have learned, things can always be worse, and I try not to stress the small stuff.

Hudson Valley Community College has definitely benefited from having Lou as a student. Not only is he an excellent student, he works with the disability services to help ensure the campus is safe and accommodating for other students who may need services. I have also seen on many occasions, where a student will be lost, or confused about classes, or what have you, and Lou will jump right in and try to help out.

He was a great asset to this school, and will always be a dear friend to me.

The Second Semester

In my second semester (spring 2016), I had four classes: Business Communications, Entrepreneurial Process, Intermediate Algebra, and Principles of Marketing.

Business Communications was where I first learned about effective communication within the workplace. This course was project-based, so I had two "big" projects for the course: my first was a forty-five-minute presentation on a topic that our group chose.

With the forty-five-minute presentation, we were split into groups. We all then set out to work on gathering enough material to fill our respective forty-five minutes. In my group, we had a student whose family was in the funeral home business, so we decided to do a presentation on the decline of the funeral home business.

After we all figured out what our topics were for our presentations, our professor put the names of each presentation on large pieces of paper. During our next class, he passed them out to us and instructed us to write questions that we had related to the topic on the paper so that group had something to go off of in terms of where they wanted to go with their research.

I was in charge of the economical side of the decline of the funeral home business. The information that I found actually surprised me because I didn't realize that the market was as saturated as it was, which was just one factor in the decline of the funeral home business.

For example, one article that I found showed me the number of deaths annually, the number of existing funeral homes, compared to the number of needed funeral homes. Pennsylvania had the highest number of unnecessary funeral homes.

The website showed that Pennsylvania had **124,596** deaths annually. They had **1,585** funeral homes to account for those deaths, but they only required **498** funeral homes to account for them.[5] That was a surplus of **1,087** funeral homes. Even though the death data was taken from 2012 and the funeral home data was taken from 2013, that is still a 218.27% increase in the number of funeral homes — which I thought was fascinating.

Pennsylvania, however, was not the highest number in terms of funeral home surpluses. Another example is Iowa. In that state, there are **27,745** deaths annually. They had **397** funeral homes to account for those deaths, but they only require **111** funeral homes to account for them.[6] That is a **257.66%** increase in the number of funeral homes!

The second presentation for the class was our final project: we had to make (or remake) a brochure for something. I chose to create one for Apple, Inc. This presentation was only a five-minute presentation, but it was just as nerve-wracking as the first presentation that we did, although that one was a bit *more* nerve-wracking because of how long it was.

Entrepreneurial Process was the second degree-specific course that I had to take. This course went over the different parts of a business plan, piece by piece from the Executive Summary all the way down to the Appendices.

For the final project of this course, we were finally able to write a business plan. For this plan, I created a business called "Lou's Wheelchair Helpers."

Intermediate Algebra reared its head again. This semester was my second time taking this course because, as I said in the last chapter, I dropped out the first time so that I wouldn't fail a class within my first semester.

This time around, I chose the teacher that I took the course with on the recommendation of my mother and sister. My sister had taken the course the previous semester with this same teacher and she had a positive result, so she thought that I would, too.

Principles of Marketing was a challenging course for me. For some reason, I could wrap my brain around the information given to me in my Entrepreneurship courses, such as in Entrepreneurial Process,) but when it came to marketing, I was next to clueless. This course was my introduction to the dreaded "B" on my transcript. I've always been a perfectionist, so seeing anything but an "A" didn't make me happy.

For the final project of this course, we had to do a marketing plan for Pepsi Next, which was a failed product of PepsiCo. that was introduced into test markets in 2011, introduced into the full launch of the product in 2012, and discontinued in 2015.[7] Sadly, because Pepsi Next is no longer available, the only source that I could find on this was on Wikipedia.

It didn't take me long to realize the reason why it was PepsiCo failed with this product: they were cannibalizing their other products by internally competing with them with a lower-calorie soft drink.

. . . .

One day, I went to check my college email and realized that I had received one from the Vice President for Academic Affairs, informing me that, because of my GPA that semester, I had been chosen for induction into Phi Theta Kappa, which is the Academic Honors Society for two-year colleges.

I was elated because I was being recognized for my hard work, but I was also nervous because there was an induction ceremony, and at the time, I didn't like going up in front of people, even if I didn't have to speak.

When I started my first semester in college, it was the first time I didn't have an aide with me; I was on my own in terms of transferring from class to class. The first semester was rather easy to transition, but as the winter set in, it was a completely different story because I had to not only battle oncoming students, but also Mother Nature — who was not at all forgiving.

Some days, I battled only snow and ice; other days, strong winds as well. The winds were so bad some days I wasn't sure if I would be able to get to class, but one way or another, I made it, even though I was late a lot of the time. The worst part, though, was that this didn't happen only once; it happened multiple times throughout the semester.

My dad had been working with my doctors at Shriners Hospital in Springfield, Massachusetts, along with our insurance company, to get me a power-wheelchair. After months of going back and forth, the insurance company came back with a notice that they would not pay for the chair until I did a "driving test" to make sure that I could successfully maneuver one on my own.

THE THIRD SEMESTER

In my third semester (fall 2016), I had four classes: Organization and Management, Statistics, Legal Issues in Entrepreneurship, and Entrepreneurial Finance.

Organization and Management was on campus. This course taught us how to go about managing the workplace, how to be a good employee, as well as how to be a good manager. This course was another project-based course, much like Business Communications. We had to do another forty-five-minute presentation, but this time, the presentation had to be on a business, as opposed to in Business Communications where we could do the project on anything that we wanted to do it on.

With the forty-five-minute presentation, we were again split into groups. We worked together to come up with a forty-five-minute presentation on a company of our choice. After we all figured out what our topics were for our presentations, our professor again put the names of each presentation on large pieces of paper. During our next class, he passed them out to us and instructed us to write questions that we had related to the topic on the paper so that group had something to go off of in terms of where they wanted to go with their research.

For this project, my group chose to talk about two organizations: Double H Ranch® and the Make-A-Wish Foundation®. Since I had been going there for the past thirteen years, I took on the part about Double H, while the rest of my group took on the Make-A-Wish Foundation®, as I didn't know much about that one, and one of my fellow group mates had a contact within Make-A-Wish, just like I had a few contacts at Ranch that I could go to.

Unlike the last semester, to get the questions answered for this particular project, we came up with interview questions and interviewed a representative from Double H and Make-A-Wish. Even though I had been going to the camp for thirteen years at that point, I was still surprised at some of the information that was given to me in the answers to the questions that I posed to them.

So, I put that, along with the information to answer the other questions that we had, in the PowerPoint, and my part was finished.

During one day in the Library, our professor came in to check on us to see how our research was going, if we had any questions that we needed clarification on, or if we wanted him to look over our interview questions (which he highly recommended.) We talked to him about our idea to interview both organizations for this project, and he told us that he had a former student who was granted a wish by Make-A-Wish. This student used the money to go to Italy with this professor's other class, International and Intercultural Business, which I will talk about more in the next chapter.

The final project for this course was a mock interview. We had to bring in a job ad for a job that we wanted to apply for as well as a copy of our resume. In preparation for this final exam, we were given a list of prospective questions that could be asked during an interview, where some were asked by the interviewer, and then we had to, in turn, interview the student who came up with us, so we had experience being the interviewee as well as the interviewer, which I liked because my degree program was Entrepreneurship, and when I start my company, I may be hiring people onto my team, so I will have to know what questions to ask, as well as which questions are considered "illegal" questions, so I don't ask those during an interview.

Statistics was taught online or on-campus. I chose to take it online because I thought it would be easier than taking it on-campus, due to the fact that I'm not very good at math. It psyches me out to be in a math test on campus, especially when it's Statistics, because I didn't really understand it that well. The outcome that I had with the course was probably because of the wonderful teacher that I took for it. She was very helpful when it came to me seeking help. Even though I took her course online, I still went to campus for Organization and Management and Entrepreneurial Finance, so I was able to get help from her in person, as well as online—which is a plus when you are not very good at Math to begin with.

To be completely honest, though, there was another reason why I took her section of the course. I had called her the previous semester to inquire about it, and she allowed me to come into her office and meet her. She said that she would walk me through the course so I would know what to expect when the time came that the course was opened for me. During our talk, though, she informed me that she didn't hold a final exam for her section—which was the "another reason" why I took her course.

Legal Issues in Entrepreneurship was one of those courses that is only offered online, and is only taught by one professor. This professor is a lawyer and is "by the book." When you don't get something in, you automatically get a grade of zero. It doesn't matter if you have an extenuating circumstance or not, you still get a zero.

I actually had two assignments in which I received zeros, but that's because I underestimated the deadline and thought it was due a week *after* it was actually due. My advice for you is to keep a copy of your course syllabi with you *at all times*, no matter if it is an online, or an on-campus class. Your syllabus is your contract between you and your professor for the successful completion of your coursework. If there are no unforeseen circumstances, your syllabus is exactly how the course will progress through the semester.

That was a wakeup call to me and helped me to be more cognizant of my online classes in the future.

Entrepreneurial Finance was taught on-campus. This course is another example of a course that only has one section with one professor. This course was the longest one that I had ever taken in my college career: an hour and fifty minutes. This class almost wasn't going to run because it only had six students in it—that's all that was in my degree program at the time. We had only six students going through it when I was to take it. To have a course run at the College, there must be seven or more students enrolled in the course.

Because it was in danger of being cancelled due to "insufficient enrollment," our professor went to our Department Chair and told him that the course should run, that the students needed it in order to graduate—so he made sure that it ran, and I was able to complete that portion of my degree.

During my time in the course, we talked about different statements related to a business:

- An income statement

- A balance sheet

- A statement of cash flow

You can also have each of the aforementioned statements at a personal level, and they work the same way: to keep track of how much money is coming in (income statement); whether you have enough income to cover your liabilities (balance sheet); and how much money is coming in vs. where it is going every month (statement of cash flow.)

We also learned about different formulas, including the Break Even Point, Horizontal Analysis of an Income Statement, and Vertical Analysis of an Income Statement. We learned what they were, why they are integral to business, and how to calculate them, and what the numbers meant that were generated by them.

. . . .

This semester was also a great one because on April 30, 2016, I took a trip with one of the clubs on campus to the Bronx Zoo, to which I hadn't been to in over five years. I went with one of the college's many clubs on a sunny Saturday and it was beautiful!

. . . .

After this semester ended and the summer began, the happiness changed to great sadness.

I endured the loss of a classmate of mine who passed away in the summer of 2016. Another classmate of ours actually shared the late classmate's obituary on my Facebook page.

For me, that would have been the only way that I found out about it because of my being in Tennessee. Sometimes, I find Facebook to be a nuisance, but other times I find it invaluable, like for telling people that they had lost a classmate if they are in a different state.

My Department Chair met with his parents after his passing to give them his business plan that he was creating through his time earning his degree at our alma mater.

That spring, the college held a memorial service for all people associated with the college who had passed away in the last year. There were twenty-seven people altogether remembered at that service from current students, employees, alumni, and friends of the college. I cannot say that I did not shed a tear, because I would be lying if I did. I didn't really have much time to process the death of my friend properly since it happened during the summer and then I had to go back to school a few weeks later.

That service helped bring closure to the loss of my classmate, although it is still a hard thing to come to terms with. It took me a few weeks to "get used to" the fact that he wasn't roaming the halls anymore. It was weird not seeing him in any more of my classes; it was weird not saying hi to him in the hallway.

The last time that I talked to the student face-to-face was in my Department Chair's office when I went in to talk to him about a final grade. We talked a few minutes together and then he had to leave—I did not know that that would be the last time I would see him.

Some of you may know the person that I am talking about. Some of you may have been in a class or two with him. Some of you may have been friends with him. Whether we know it or not, I think that we all have been impacted by this young man in one way or another. I know that I have been. I had found not only a classmate that I clicked well with in class, but also a friend.

The classmate that I am talking about is Sean Craig. He passed away on July 31, 2016. He was a bright student who always had a smile on his face. He brightened up the day of anyone who met him. I will forever be grateful for my interactions with Sean because he has helped me be a better person.

The college has a memorial service every spring semester for all of the people who have passed away in the previous year. Because Sean was one of those students, our Department Chair, Ricky Thibodeau, was asked by Sean's parents to speak at the service. His full eulogy follows:

"Hello, my name is Ricky Thibodeau. I'm the Department Chair here at HVCC within the School of Business. Outside of my administrative responsibilities, I also teach and was fortunate to have Sean Craig as one of my students. Sean was enrolled in our Entrepreneurship program and was also a member of our entrepreneurship club. He was a 4.0 student and was very involved with activities here at Hudson Valley and formed very strong bonds with all his fellow classmates and professors — <u>including myself</u>.

It will be a year ago this July that we all felt the pain of losing such a wonderful young man. When I heard the news from the college, I was working on my log cabin deep in the Adirondacks. It was an instant feeling of pain, numbness, and disbelief that continues to this day. I immediately stopped what I was doing, packed my bags and went home that afternoon although I was not planning on going back home for a few days. Being a father myself, I needed to get home to my own kids and hug my daughter and son and tell them how much I loved them. Since they are teenagers, they of course just brush you off with these hugs because it's "embarrassing" but I just needed that. I'm sure all the parents here know what I mean.

Although I had only known Sean for two semesters here at Hudson Valley, I grew very close to him due to our many discussions. He enrolled in my Entrepreneurial Process class for the spring 2016 term. Before he started my class, I got to know him his first semester at HVCC since he sought me out since I'm chair of the department and he wanted to talk about his ideas. Sean had several ideas.

I remember the first time we spoke he mentioned he enjoyed paintball, and he wanted to incorporate the elements of paintball into a ninja warrior course. We would come up with these crazy ways to implement this plan with certain obstacles, trampolines, and so on, all the while you had someone firing paintballs at you. We laughed often talking about this and soon realized it may not be a sustainable business so [we] moved on to other ideas. Sean finally settled on a Stand-Up Paddleboard business for the Adirondacks which is the project he worked on the entire semester and wrote a business plan for it. With his perseverance, positive attitude, people skills, and work ethic, there is no doubt he would have been successful. Today I presented his business plan to his parents. There is not a day this semester that I don't think of Sean. I'm teaching the same course in the same classroom and every day I walk into that classroom, I have images of Sean sitting there in the second row, three seats back, positive and always smiling. He was always there and never missed a class.

Each day after class, Sean would either approach the front to chat or he would follow me to my office so we could discuss more ideas he had. It didn't take long that our chats turned personal and we would talk about our mutual love for the outdoors, boating, fishing, hunting, hiking, and the love we had for our cats. We chatted about the Adirondacks all the time and would compare my area to his area stating why one was better than the other. We solved that argument by inviting each other to their respective lakes for the upcoming summer. I'm certain we would have had some laughs and not even cared which area is better since it's the company you're with that makes it special.

There were several qualities that I valued in Sean and the one quality I valued the most was how our chats turned to his family. He talked about his mom and dad all the time, including working with his dad at Alpin Haus. Ron, just so you know, he also had quite a few ideas about doing things differently at Alpin Haus. He loved his job there and loved working with you. He was the youngest of three boys, I was the youngest of three boys so we would talk about the challenges of being the youngest and how the big brothers whom we would fight with often growing up became the big brothers that we later loved and looked up to. I'm a firm believer that your family has the greatest influence on you growing up and makes you into who you are today.

Over the course of the last year, I have been fortunate to get to know Ron and Theresa better and now I have finally met them in person including Sean's beloved grandmother. There's no doubt the influence Sean's family had on him had created these strong values this young man had. He was a <u>remarkable young man</u> with <u>incredible values</u> who had a bright future ahead of him. I was honored to have known him."

When asked to reflect about Sean; his parents, Theresa and Ron, had this to say:

"Spring Semester 2017 at HVCC. We arrived on campus with so many mixed feelings and emotions. We should have been preparing for Sean's graduation the following month, but instead, we were there for a memorial service for students, faculty, and staff that had passed away. It had been nine months since we lost Sean. How could it be that we were there for this event? We were still so numb and heartbroken. For me, as his mom, coming to campus had been even more meaningful as an alumni, class of 1976, how could I be returning to my alma mater to honor my deceased child?

Sean loved college and finished his first year with a 4.0 and a spot on the President's List. He was majoring in Entrepreneurship and had already submitted a business plan for one of his courses. School never came easy for him. He had to work harder than others but he was determined and gave it his all. His bright smile and fun, lovely personality were the light and love of our lives.

Sadly, his life was cut short while on summer break. We received correspondence and calls from a number of professors and the administration to express their condolences. Some had very personal stories to share about their positive experience of having had Sean as their student and were deeply saddened by the news of his death. We were consoled by the wonderful things they shared about Sean. They told us to expect an invitation to the memorial service in the spring and hoped we could attend.

Our family was joined by Sean's best friend and college roommate along with his other dear friends who were attending nearby colleges. There was a sad, surreal sense about it, but at the same time, we could feel Sean's positive spirit holding us up. We were approached by two of Sean's professors who had reached out to us previously to offer words of sympathy and support. They continued to talk about Sean's outgoing personality and how they enjoyed having him in their class.

The service was very reverent, with soothing music and touching scripture readings. They read aloud the name of each person who had passed and we participated as family members were invited to place a flower, in memory of their loved one, in a vase at the front of the auditorium. Then came the personal eulogies. Sean's professor and department head, who had only known our son for nine months, talked about him as if he were a member of our family. We were overcome with pride as he spoke about Sean's academic accomplishments, personal interests they shared, and the love our son expressed for his family and friends back home. It meant so much to us!

After the service, we gathered for a reception and expressed our gratitude to all those who came to honor Sean. We offered condolences to others and although we were strangers to each other, our common bond was loss and grief. In the case of students who were being remembered, there was the added sadness of young lives cut short. In some cases, for surviving classmates, it was their first experience with the death of a friend their own age.

We were blessed by one more encounter that day. At one point, a young man approached us to introduce himself as Sean's classmate and offer his condolences. The sadness in his face and voice told the story of someone who was impacted by having established personal connection to our son. Meeting Louis and staying friends with him, we can now see why Sean befriended him. They shared the gift of perseverance and "grit"! We left the college on that day feeling that our son, Sean, had graduated with high honors."

Sean taught me something that I have taken with me and held close to my heart ever since: if you have a little determination, you can do anything you set your mind to. That rang in my mind throughout the remaining semesters at my alma mater, and still rings true today. He is one of the many things that drives me today to continue pursuing my dreams. He had big dreams but was unable to pursue them due to a life cut short. I live my life every day striving to make him proud.

. . . .

Following this chapter is a piece by Andrew F. Roberts. He's an academic coach who came to my alma mater when one of the academic coaches resigned. I struck up a conversation with him in his first few days, and he told me that he had a degree in Communications—we jokingly refer to it as a "degree in talking." Since he was new, I had to make sure that he realized that I'm a hard worker. He was a pivotal part of my semesters from the time that he came, to the end of fall 2017, especially when it came to my Public Speaking class.

Persistence

by Andrew F. Roberts

I spent a lot of time thinking what to write about Lou. To anyone who knows him, it is pretty obvious that it is hard to break down Lou as a person into a small written piece. However, when it came to titling my piece, that was the easy part. "Persistence" is easily the best word I could use to describe Lou.

In first coming to HVCC, I did not know what to expect. It was my first time working at an institution in New York, my first community college, and my first time working in a smaller office of only three full-time staff members. Needless to say, the first day what a blur. However, one thing I remember clearly is Lou coming in to speak to me and simply asking about me. He was persistent in his quest to learn about the "new guy". It didn't take long to learn that this was Lou's modus operandi.

Lou showed me how persistent a student really can be. Whether it was a simple homework assignment or an end of semester capstone speech, Lou put his heart into every single assignment. I've worked with Lou through times of anger, tears, frustration, and (when almost every assignment came back with an "A" grade) happiness. Lou helped set the standard for persistence in even the toughest academic situations.

Personally, I have grown through meeting and working with Lou in a few different ways. Aside from the aforementioned understanding of how persistent a student can be, Lou showed how perseverance can transform a student experience, specifically for those with a physical disability. Lou has forged a path for those with physical disabilities to come on campus, and the impact that he has left on the faculty and staff will undoubtedly find itself transferring to new students who pass through the doors of Hudson Valley Community College. Although Lou's graduation was a loss to the campus community, I believe it is safe to say that his impact on HVCC is far from over.

THE PENULTIMATE SEMESTER: MY FOURTH SEMESTER

In my fourth semester (spring 2017), I had four classes: Personal Finance, International and Intercultural Business, Spanish Language and Culture I, and Entrepreneurial Strategy.

Personal Finance was one of the best courses that I took at Hudson Valley, and it was all because of the professor that I chose to take the course with. The semester before I took this course, I talked to one of the professors' husbands, and he recommended that I take her for the course because he thought that I would greatly benefit from having her as my professor, and he was right.

I had taken three of the husband's courses before this time, so he and I had a great rapport going. I trusted his recommendation, and I'm glad that I did, not just because of all I learned in the classroom, but because I gained another friend, another person behind me on this crazy journey through college, and I am forever grateful to her for all she taught me during the course, and her friendship.

This professor was actually the wife of the professor with whom I took Business Communications, Organization and Management, International and Intercultural Business, and Organizational Leadership with. I was introduced to her the semester before while she was talking to her husband in the hallway of one of the buildings on campus.

While I was in the course with her, we went over a few chapters of the book (if my memory serves, we only went up to the chapter on financial statements), and then she assigned the final project, and we worked on that for the remainder of the semester.

The final project was a fifteen-year cash flow plan, starting in 2017. We had to plan out all of our expenses from a house, to a car, to personal care products. The good thing about this plan was that it was different for everyone; there was no one-size-fits-all mentality with this assignment as everyone's situation is different which, in my opinion, made the project that much more fun.

. . . .

For the successful completion of my degree requirements, I had to pick two classes that satisfy two electives: one free elective and one liberal arts elective. For my free elective, I chose to take International and Intercultural Business, and for my liberal arts elective, I chose to take Spanish Language and Culture I.

International and Intercultural Business is an eight-week late-Sprint course offered in the spring semester.

For the course itself, I was asked to do article summaries just about every week on various topics, comment on what I learned from a PDF that our professor had provided in the course and, for our final project, write a one to two-page paper on what I learned in Italy that I could not have learned in a classroom environment.

Although our class was online, we met twice in person in a classroom on campus because our professor thought that it was good for us to meet before the three weeks in Italy.

We met twice during the semester before our trip. In those meetings, our professor told us what to expect while in Italy, and we also talked with students who had previously taken the trip. They all said it was wonderful, that we would love it. One thing that he told us to do was bring our eyeglass prescription because there was an eyeglass shop in the Alps where we could get glasses at a much lower price than in the States.

The course ran from March 12 to May 12, 2017. We were off to Venice on May 16, 2017. Our flight was out of J.F.K. Airport with Aer Lingus, which is based out of the Ireland. We were supposed to leave J.F.K. at 5:30pm Eastern Standard Time, but we didn't end up getting into the air until about 5:50 pm, although we *did* make up time in the air, so that was a good thing. We had a two-hour layover in Dublin, Ireland, which was just enough time to get to our connecting flight, and then we were off to Venice.

Traveling to Venice, the flight times were approximately seven hours for the first flight and three and a half hours for the second, due to the fact that we were traveling with, not against the Jet Stream.

Normally, on an American flight, when it comes in, the people with disabilities, or who required extra time and/or assistance getting onto the flight and into their seats are supposed to be boarded first, but on this particular flight, the plane had to be refueled once it got into J.F.K. Granted, I know that's not their fault, but what happened was that people who were able-bodied were able to be boarded, and the people with disabilities, or who required extra time and/or assistance getting onto the flight and into their seats were told that they had to wait until after the plane was fueled. Both my professor and I found that very odd.

When we got to Venice at about 3:00 pm Central European Standard Time (CEST), we got off the plane, retrieved our bags, and our professor bought our tickets for the Alilaguna—which was a waterbus that went from the airport to the islands within the Venetian Lagoon—and then we went to our destination where our bed and breakfast was: The Lido. While on the Alilaguna, our professor did tell us when he gave us our tickets for the waterbus and the Alilaguna, was that we should keep them in a safe place because if we did not have them, we could be fined.

Once we disembarked the Alilaguna onto the Lido, we only had about five hundred feet to walk to get to our bed and breakfast that we were staying at for the first week. Once there, we gave our passports to the hotel manager to check us in, and we went off to pick our rooms. I got room three, which was to the left of the main doorway (which made it easy to go in and out of the bed and breakfast during the day and come back at night).

Once we reached our bed and breakfast, we gave our passports to the hotel manager. Once we were checked-in, we were able to pick what rooms we slept in for the first week, and then unpacked our bags. After we were unpacked, our professor showed us around the Lido.

During our first week in Italy, my friends went rowing. Because of my disability, I was unable to go with them. Since I could not go with them, I sat and watched the first day, but the other two times that my classmates went out on the boats, I went with a friend of mine, and she showed me around some of the different churches in Venice. One of the churches that she showed me was La Chiesa di Sant'Alvise, or The Church of St. Alvise.

One of the things that she told me as we were entering the church was that Alvise is Venetian for Luigi. Luigi is Italian for Louis. So, in a sense, I am named after an Italian saint, *and* I have a church named for me. I thought that was really neat.

While in the church, I was unable to take any physical photographs, only the photos that I took with my mind's camera. That's because the flash of the camera (which is often needed in various areas, such as that particular church, and *Basilica di San Marco*, St. Mark's Basilica, as another example), would slowly erode the beautiful architecture of the building.

When we were in the Alps, my classmates and I took a bike down a trail to Austria. Because I couldn't use the bicycles, though, my professor thought of an alternative: to have me in my wheelchair and he rollerbladed down the trail — which was really fun! On that trip, we met a horse who followed us for a few feet, until he couldn't anymore due to the constraints of the fence he was behind. He kept talking to us while we were resting, trying to strike up a conversation!

Another day while in the Alps, we visited an Olympic Ski Jump. It was really neat to see how tall and long it was! (And, although I had been skiing for thirteen years beforehand, I didn't, and still don't, think that I am capable of scaling something like that!)

We also visited an eyeglass shop while in the Alps. I found a pair of glasses that were a lot lighter on my face than the ones that I was wearing. I didn't even realize the weight of the ones I had been wearing until I had tried on the new ones! Needless to say, those came home with me, along with a pair of sunglasses. All in all, they cost me €240,00 EUR (which, at the time, equated to about $264.00 USD).

It's not possible to explain every single thing that we did while over in Italy, but to sum it up: it was a once in a lifetime experience—although I do want to go back again. While over there, I had sense of belonging. Like I said earlier in this section, our professor told us that the people over in Italy were waiting for us, and he was right. Now, they are waiting for me to come back.

As I talked about earlier in this section, for the final project, we were asked to write a one to two-page paper on what I learned in Italy that I could not have learned in a classroom environment. Those were the only requirements for the paper, so we could pretty much talk about anything that we wanted to within the paper.

For example, some of the things that I learned were:

1. That the toilets are different in Italy then in America;

2. That it is rude to not begin eating as soon as you are served;

3. A few words in Italian and a few words in the Venetian dialect;

4. That people say "Pronto" when answering the phone;

5. That it is somewhat easier to acclimate to time changes then I thought it would be;

6. Your classmates and your professor can quickly become your family, if you allow them to; if you let loose a little, you will have great fun.

To flush the toilets, there is a "button" (of sorts) above the toilet that you press, instead of a silver handle that is common in the United States.

When I had my first piece of food, I waited for others to be served before I started eating. My professor saw that, and then told me that it was rude to not start eating as soon as you were served.

While going around Italy, I learned a few words in Italian that I did not know previously: buongiorno and buonasera, and used those regularly when greeting others. I also learned early on about the various dialects that are spoken in Italy. I was brought up speaking a Sicilian dialect, while everyone where we were in the Northern part of Italy spoke Venetian. "Come va?" was one of the things that I learned early on in terms of how to say "How are you?"

When picking up the phone, I heard people saying "pronto" as a greeting. I learned quickly that that meant "I'm ready to talk."

I also learned that it is somewhat easier to acclimate to time changes then I had originally thought it was. I thought that we would be unable to wake up feeling rested the first few days, but it was possible for some people — either that, or they are just great actors!

One of the best things that I learned on the trip is how quickly your classmates, and your professor, can become your family. When we were in Italy, our relationships as students and professor (and student to student) changed: We let our guards down and talked to each other as people, more about our families and less about the actual school and grades and all that goes with it. We were with each other for twenty-one, almost twenty-two days, so of course we got close. We have created lasting bonds, not only with each other, but with our Italian friends as well, and those are what matter the most: the connections, the bonds that were established.

I learned rather quickly while writing that paper that it would be hard to condense three weeks' worth of learning into two pages. So, I found that I could only pick a few of the things that I learned.

Our professor told us that he wanted to make the course one that we would remember for a long time, and he did. It was a once in a lifetime experience, although I cannot wait to go back to visit the many friends that I made while there.

Spanish Language and Culture I was an introduction into the Spanish language and culture of Spanish speaking countries. The course is geared toward people who do not have any knowledge of Spanish, but it had been so long since I took Spanish that I had asked my academic advisor if I could take Spanish I because I was unsure if I was going to remember everything I learned years ago, and I was afraid that I would fail the course — which I do not like to do. Heck, I don't even like getting a "B" on my transcript!

So, to hopefully not get another "B" on my transcript (since I already had two of them, I took Spanish Language and Culture I, and I actually *did* learn things, even though I had taken the class before. For example: they changed the Spanish alphabet. They no longer consider the "CH" or the "LL" ('double L', as it was called) as part of the alphabet. Other than that, they kept the rest of the alphabet the same. When I first learned of this, I was surprised that they changed it. I knew that there may be changes, but I didn't realize that they were so drastic as to changing the alphabet of the Spanish language itself.

A few weeks later, after midterms, we were given a project in which we had to create a PowerPoint presentation on a Spanish speaking country. My project partner and I were assigned Panama. We only had to create the presentation in English, but me being the overachiever, I created it in Spanish as well (for my own satisfaction).

When it came time to take quizzes and unit tests, I was rather hard on myself when I received the grade back because I had taken Spanish I in middle school and received a ninety-one percent on that final exam. I thought that getting anything under a hundred percent on an exam in that class was unacceptable—as if I had failed.

My professor told me multiple times not to be so hard on myself because everyone makes mistakes, and we are all human. We are not perfect, and we cannot get everything one hundred percent correct all the time.

Entrepreneurial Strategy was what is called the "capstone" course of my degree program. This type of class is where we apply everything we learned in the previous degree-required classes (Introduction to Entrepreneurship, Entrepreneurial Process, Entrepreneurial Finance, and Legal Issues in Entrepreneurship) to create a semester-long project, which was a thirty-plus page business plan.

Luckily, we didn't have to start from the beginning; we could use the plans that we had created in previous classes (such as in Entrepreneurial Process, for example). I chose to do this, instead of reinventing the wheel and attempting to come up with another project altogether. I thought that that would be more of an undertaking than attempting to further one that I had been working on for the past two semesters.

The project that I chose to do was for a fictitious business called Lou's Wheelchair Helpers. This is a company that licenses out the idea for an add-on accessory for a manual wheelchair to help it get up steep ramps. The idea of the mechanism is to make it so the wheelchair and the user within it does not roll backward down the ramp when their arms get tired from wheeling up it.

The mechanisms are on either side of the wheel-chair and, when a button is pressed, they are supposed to come out of their curled-up positions on either side of the chair and attach via claws, like the claw machines that you see in arcades and other places.

To write the business plan itself, we had assign-ments that we had to write up and hand in each week, and by the end of the semester, by putting each of the pieces together, we had the full business plan. Normally everything for an online class is submitted online through the course, but for this particular project, our professor told us that we had to hand it into her in person in her office by Friday, May 12, 2017 at 3:00 pm. We also had to schedule two appointments with our professor during the semester so that she could check-in with us on our progress on the plan.

While I was going through the plan, I found that there were a few pieces that were challenging to complete and write for the plan. One such part of the plan was the Feasibility Analysis, which tells you whether it is feasible to go forward with the venture you are wanting to start. If it is, and you have all of your ducks in a row, then good for you, go ahead! But, it will also show you where you lack, what you need to work on before you make your venture a reality. It took me three weeks to get this assignment completed, and that was with the help of a Librarian with a string of Individual Library Instruction appointments. It took about three or four appointments to get this particular piece of the project completed because of its complexity.

To complete this project, we used a variety of sources, including ReferenceUSA and Statista. Statista is used when you are wanting to look up statistics on something. For example, we used it to see if we could find any trends for the wheelchair manufacturer industry. We found a graph of wheelchair manufacturers, and a heat map of where they were located. We were surprised to find that in recent years, wheelchair manufacturers were heavily concentrated within the Northeastern part of the United States.

We used the U.S. Historical Businesses section of ReferenceUSA to obtain past references to how many wheelchair manufacturers there were in the past compared to today. To do this, we had to figure out the reference code for the industry. For a while, we were looking for the NAICS code for it, but we realized that the industry is so old that it wouldn't have a NAICS code, it would have a SIC code (384213).

At the point in time that we were conducting the research, we only had up until 2015 as the most recent year of information. This research was being conducted in 2016, so it was recent, but we didn't have the information for 2016 at the point in time when we were conducting the research for the project. 2015 was as current as we could get.

The Final Salute:
My Fifth Semester

In my fifth—and final—semester (fall 2017), I had four classes: Organizational Leadership, Principles of Microeconomics, Public Speaking, and Selling and Sales Management.

In the Spring of 2016, I was advised to take Principles of Microeconomics, Public Speaking, Selling and Sales Management, and the Entrepreneurial Internship (either ENTR or BADM 290, depending on which one is open that semester; for me, it was BADM 290).

Originally, this was how my semester was supposed to go:

- Principles of Microeconomics

- Public Speaking

- Selling and Sales Management

- Entrepreneurial Internship

After my advisor told me of this, I received my Advisement Verification Number for the final time, and I was on to scheduling my classes for my final semester.

On August 24, 2017, the Thursday before classes started, I received an email from the scheduling office stating that my internship was canceled. As soon as I read that email, I was on the phone attempting to get ahold of my Department Chair, Ricky Thibodeau. He was the person who I had to go to in order to get this changed around because that's the policy, as stated on the Entrepreneurship A.A.S. degree's page on the website: "Students will be expected to participate in the Entrepreneurial Internship. In extenuating circumstances (as determined by the Department Chair), the Internship may be replaced with an elective approved by the Department Chair."[8]

I originally emailed him to tell him of the fact that my internship was canceled due to insufficient enrollment, as well as some courses that I wanted to take in place of the internship, but when I spoke with him on the phone, he said that if the internship is canceled, he had to get the course substitution approved by the then vice president for Academic Affairs. After going back and forth with him for a few minutes, after being approved the next day, Organizational Leadership was added to my schedule of classes for the fall 2017 semester.

Organizational Leadership was a fun and rewarding course to take. Per the requirements of the course, we had to complete two discussion boards per week (consisting of one original reply per discussion board in each discussion board and replies to two other student's posts). In addition to the discussion boards, we also had five article summaries that we had to complete on different things. Most times, though, we just chose one thing from the text and we had to write a minimum of three paragraphs on the article. We also had quizzes that we had to take on the weeks that we didn't have an article summary to hand in.

It depended on the week, but sometimes we had two discussion boards to complete, sometimes we had three—it depended on the week—and on whether we had an article summary to complete or not.

One of the questions that was posed to us by our professor was talking about stress in the work-place, and then we were asked what brought us stress at my alma mater.

In my answer, I talked about how the coursework from high school to college is a lot different—it may seem like you get assigned a lot more work, or you have to spend more time on your work than you did in high school.

To some extent, this is true because for some classes, you only have fifty minutes three or four days a week with your professor and you are expected to spend that time, and more, outside of class working on your assignments. Now, for some, you may require that, but not for others. It depends on the assignment, the course load and workload of the course itself.

For some classes, your professor may require you to do more work because you are unable to complete it all in your fifty minutes together. That's understandable and, most times, to be expected because of the nature of a class.

Some of the questions, though, required us to utilize the textbook to answer the question. For example, there were some discussion board questions which directed us to a questionnaire within the textbook and we had to fill it out in regard to how our employer ranked on certain things.

It was amazing to see the different answers that each of the students gave to the questions posed within the discussion board. We all had a unique perspective to offer within the course, and that was a great way to help us learn how to be excellent leaders within the workplace.

Alongside the discussion boards that we were given, we also had quizzes and article summaries that we had to complete throughout the semester. One of the article summaries was on anything within the chapter content for that week. I took one look through the chapters, and I saw a piece on Maslow's Hierarchy of Needs, so I did my article summary on that. Maslow's Hierarchy was something that I learned about in my first semester in General Psychology, and something that we briefly talked about again while our professor told us about how to write and deliver a persuasive speech.

The quizzes were twenty questions, and we had twenty minutes to complete it. Although it was timed, unlike some other quizzes that I had taken for classes in an online environment, it didn't kick you off the exam once the time was up; you were allowed to go overtime.

For the article summaries, sometimes we had to pick something from the text, find an article on it, and write a summary of that article; other times, we had to do an article summary on something our professor talked about within the module.

At the end of the semester, we had to submit a final paper that we wrote on a person whom we considered a leader. This leader was not to be someone famous, but rather someone like a baseball, football, or softball coach, or a professor that we had that we thought was a great leader — those were just some examples of people we could use for the paper, though. This was a term paper, so the requirements were available to us at the beginning of the semester. This was one of the first things that I took a look at in the first week of the course. When I was reading the requirements for the paper, the college's President, Dr. Andrew "Drew" Matonak, Ed.D., popped into my head, so I chose to do my paper on him.

Principles of Microeconomics was a challenging course. It was offered online and on-campus in the fall 2017 semester. I chose to take it online because I thought that that would be a bit easier than taking it on-campus, especially in regard to the exams. For the unit exams I was correct; for the final exam, I was not.

The exams were very challenging to complete, even though each exam was a combination of multiple choice questions and reading graphs, for the most part.

I had one exam with two questions that were basically identical, the only thing that was different were the names that my professor used for the people. I got the first one wrong, but the second one correct.

Public Speaking was a challenging course to take. I have always had a fear of speaking in front of people for a variety of reasons, but lack of confidence in myself and what I am saying is probably ranked up high on that list of things.

Throughout the semester, we had to do five "big" speeches: Introduction, Demonstrative, Informative, Persuasive, and Ceremonial. For the Introduction, Demonstrative, Informative, Persuasive speeches, we had to complete a self-evaluation afterward. For speech five, the Ceremonial Speech, we did not. For each speech, we had to have two copies of our outlines: one for us to use during our speeches, and one for our professor to use when grading our speeches.

The *Introduction Speech* was our first speech. The topic for the Introduction Speech was a music lyric. We only had about five minutes to deliver this speech, and we did not know a lot about how to write a speech at this point because this was in the very beginning of the semester.

For this speech, I chose to do "Lean on Me" by Bill Withers because of my appreciation of the song for the past fourteen years. I was supposed to pick a piece of the lyrics and talk about how it pertains to me as a person.

When it was my turn to deliver this speech, I was extremely nervous. While my professor was talking about the introduction speech, she said that we should try and not use filler words in the speech. So, what did I do? I used filler words with just about every other word that came out of my mouth. My anxiety and nervousness got so bad to where I was talking fast and losing my place in the speech outline.

Sitting back in my seat, the nervousness didn't cease—it just changed to worry about how I performed and what my grade would be. Needless to say, it wasn't what I was expecting, but it still wasn't very good, either.

This speech was the first speech of the semester. I didn't have much knowledge under my belt in the way of writing speeches, so it really wasn't very well written. I also found that when delivering the speech to my classmates that I was very nervous. I also used "filler words," such as "um," "uh," and "so" a lot when I didn't know what to say, or found that I had lost my place.

Mostly, though, the filler words were used because I was nervous, because I had a fear of public speaking. Like I said earlier in this book, I always had a fear of public speaking, and I felt that it had come forward in this speech because of my rather excessive use of filler words during the delivery.

When I received the grade for the speech, I was rather disappointed because it was the lowest grade that I had ever received on an assignment before: the grade was a "C," which is between a seventy and seventy-nine percent. Sometimes the way that Hudson Valley grades with the range like that is to the benefit of the student, and other times it is not. This time, however, it was very much a relief because if there wasn't that range, I would have most likely failed the speech—at least, that's what it feels like.

The *Demonstration Speech* was our second speech. For that speech, I chose to show people how to play the card game called "Golf." Because I could not go behind the desk in our classroom that housed the Document Camera, my professor and I had to work with the director of the Center for Access and Assistive Technology, as well as the Information Technology Services (ITS) Department.

For this speech, one of the things that was different from the introduction speech was the organization of it. The introduction speech looked as if I had outlined it myself. With the second speech, we received an outline from our professor that, if we followed it, we were sure to hit on each point that she was going to grade us on.

For my speech, I demonstrated to my class how to play the card game "Golf." I've been playing it for a few years now, and I know how to play it well, but when it came to explain it to the class when I was demonstrating it, I don't feel like I did it well.

One person who listened to my speech told me that it was confusing to follow. To be honest, I felt confused as I was demonstrating it because I let my nerves get the best of me and just about succumbed to them.

The *Informative Speech* was our third "big" speech. For the informative speech, I chose to tell my class about my trip to Italy that I took with the International and Intercultural Business course through the college in the summer of 2016. We spent three weeks in Italy: first in Venice, second in the Alps, and then back to Venice again for our final week.

If you would like to learn more about my experiences while in Italy, you can read the International and Intercultural Business entry in the spring 2016 chapter of this book.

For this speech, one of the requirements was to use a visual aid. I once again went to the Center for Access and Assistive Technology to talk to the director, and she put in another work order for the Information Technology Services (ITS) department to come and place a Document Camera onto my desk.

When it was my turn to deliver my speech, I had a visual aid set and ready to go for the speech, but I didn't end up using it because my mind was so focused on getting through the speech that I had forgotten to show it.

I realized that only after I had concluded the delivery of my speech, and I could feel chills run down my spine. My mind immediately went to the thought of, "I'm going to fail this speech..." all because I didn't show the visual aid during it.

The *Persuasive Speech* was our "final" speech, but it wasn't our "last" speech. It was during the second to last week of classes.

For this speech, we had to satisfy the five steps of Monroe's Motivated Sequences, which are Attention, Need, Solution, Visualization, and Action.

1. In the **Attention** step, we need to successfully gain the audience's attention.

2. In the **Needs** step, we need to successfully convey the need that we feel is unfulfilled.

3. For the **Solution** step, we need to find a solution that satisfies the need.

4. For the **Visualization** step, we need to create a visualization using the power of language (descriptive language is an example) to put the picture in the audience's minds of how their futures will be better if they adopt this solution.

5. For the **Action** step, we need to urge them to take action on the solution.

This speech received a "B" for a grade.

The persuasive speech was probably the most challenging speech to write for this semester. It required a lot of research as well as a lot of time to actually write the outline itself.

This speech was unique, though, because I also had to use a PowerPoint presentation and, for that, I had to use a Presentation Remote. This was the only speech in which I used a PowerPoint, so it was kind of challenging to try to sync the slides with my speech—making sure that I transitioned to the next slide when I talked about the next thing.

We had to upload our PowerPoints to a discussion board within Blackboard, and then go off of our professor's account, so we do not make any changes to the PowerPoint after the due date (since the PowerPoint was considered part of the presentation like the outlines, we are unable to change them after they are due).

For this speech, I practiced more than any of my previous ones. I had to to make sure that I stayed within the five-minute time limit because my professor said that if we went over five minutes that anything after that would not be considered for grading.

Needless to say, hearing that kind of put me on edge a little bit because of the length of my previous speeches.

So, I set out to write this speech. At the beginning, I wanted to do cremation, but then I changed my course of the speech to green burial (which is a way of caring for the dead with minimal environ-mental impact that aids in the conservation of natural resources, reduction of carbon emissions, protection of worker health, and the restoration and/or preservation of habitat. Green burial necessitates the use of non-toxic and biode-gradable materials, such as caskets, shrouds, and urns.[9]), but ultimately, I changed it back to cremation in the end.

In terms of delivering the speech, I thought at the time, and still feel that this speech was one of the better ones that I delivered, in terms of the ones that I already have: the Introduction, Demonstrative, and Informative Speeches.

After our persuasive speeches were complete, we had one more to complete: our ceremonial speeches.

The *Ceremonial Speech* was our last speech of the semester. For that, we got to choose what we wanted to do from the six ceremonial speech subjects that were outlined in class, although when I looked on Blackboard for the requirements, it looked like we had to choose from either an introduction speech, a toast, or a eulogy, so I chose to do a toast.

Who did I do a toast to, you may ask? Well, none other than the Jolly Old Elf himself: Santa Claus! It was probably the most fun speech that I had written because I could be creative. The other four speeches had strict parameters on what needed to be there (such as Monroe's Motivated Sequence for the Persuasion Speech). This speech was delivered during the final week of classes.

This speech received an "A" for a grade. This was the highest grade that I had received on any of my speeches that I wrote and delivered for this course. I'd be lying if I said I wasn't happy about that. In the whole course, I strived for perfection, but when I saw the "C" grade on the first speeches, that just about killed my confidence for the course.

I mentioned in my Persuasive Speech commentary that that speech was probably better than the previous speeches that I had written/delivered, and I hold to that, but in terms of ease to write it, I feel that the ceremonial speech was probably the easiest to write because there wasn't any research that had to be done for it, there were no verbal citations like there were in my other speeches.

Writing this speech was relatively easy, once I knew what I was going to write the speech on. When I was assigned this speech, I wrote it in about a day. I was told not to stress over it, to have fun, and be creative with it, so I was. Like it says within the speech outline, I decided to do a toast to Santa Claus.

My thought process for the subject of this speech was rather simple: it was around Christmas Time, so what better way to bring the joy by doing a toast to the Jolly Old Elf himself?

When I delivered the speech to my class, I started out my speech with "He sees you when you're sleeping. He knows when you're awake. He knows if you've been bad or good, so be good for goodness sake!" and everyone immediately knew who the speech was about before I went further. I saw smiles come on the faces of my classmates, and heard a few laughs, too. I was overjoyed at the reactions I was getting, especially considering nothing like that happened in any of my previous speeches. I was happy to be able to finally connect with my audience.

Looking back, if I could do my degree over again, I would take Business Communications and Public Speaking in the same semester because I feel that my Public Speaking course could help with the presentation that I had to do within Business Communications.

Selling and Sales Management was another course where there was only one section offered by one professor, so you don't have any choice in who to take the course with, like you do in some other courses, such as Public Speaking, for example.

I had to use the textbook a lot, as you have to in a lot of online courses. Every week, we either had a small "paper" due or we had a discussion board to post in.

The papers were just small assignments in which we had to read small pieces of each chapter and answer questions on what we read.

For the discussion board, I had to write my own, original post answering the question that was posed and then respond to one other student in a reply to their post.

The final exam of the course was three questions that gave hypothetical scenarios and we had to figure out the compensation packages for each.

At the end of the semester, I checked my grades and noticed that I earned a 3.75 cumulative GPA. I received my degree and certificate of Honors in the mail on January 30, 2018. I graduated with Honors at the 64th Commencement Ceremony on May 12, 2018.

. . . .

Following this chapter, I have pieces from two faculty members from Hudson Valley: John

Meehan and Dr. Valerie Lang Waldin, J.D., M.L.S., Associate Professor/Librarian.

John Meehan is an associate professor at my alma mater. The first of many courses that I took with him was his Business Communications course.

Little did I know how much value I would get out of his courses, and out of him as a professor. He wasn't only my professor, though, he was also my friend. A friend that I would go to for more than just questions about his course(s) that I was taking with him. We talked about our families, interests that we had in common (like skiing!), as well as Tennessee, which my family had been traveling to for about a decade by the time that I had met John. We loved it so much to where we wanted to move there.

One of the important things that John taught me was to break out of my comfort zone. I did that a lot while in Italy with him and my classmates in his International and Intercultural Business course.

Through that course, John helped reinforce in me what Sean taught me all those semesters before: if you have a little determination, you can do anything you set your mind to. Italy was a place I always wanted to go, but not something that I thought was attainable. With his help, it was. With his help, I was able to bust out of my shell. I was able to forget that I had a disability, because the people that I met in Italy didn't see me as that; they saw me as a regular kid.

I'm grateful to John for allowing me to go, for helping me out of my shell. I'm forever changed for the better because of my experiences in Italy, and it's all thanks to him, my classmates, and my friends in Italy.

Dr. Valerie Lang Waldin, J.D., M.L.S., Associate Professor/Librarian is an associate professor and librarian in the Dwight Marvin Library who specializes in business and economics. Dr. Waldin is a wonderful human being with a heart of gold, and an affinity for animals. She was quick to help me with any assignment in which I needed help with.

I first met her when I required help on my final project for my Entrepreneurial Process course in the spring 2016 semester. Little did I know, that one meeting cultivated a beautiful friendship.

I'm grateful for her countless hours of help throughout my time earning my degree, as well as for being a wonderful friend I can always count on.

COLLEGE AND BEYOND

by John Meehan

I first met Louis in August of 2016, just several months after his HVCC adventure began. Louis and I hit it off right from the start, so much so that he ended up taking four classes with me as his instructor. I feel honored to have had the opportunity to work with Louis over the past two years and I feel that I have learned as much from him as he has learned from me, maybe more.

The first time I met Louis I was impressed with his mature attitude and his professionalism. These attributes became even more apparent to me in the semesters in which he took BADM 200, Business Communications and BADM 207, Organization & Management. Louis and his project team members really did a fantastic job in each class in their forty-five-minute presentations. Seeing Louis in both of these classes three days a week furthered our student/instructor bond. Louis would often stop by my office in the morning and we would talk about school, but more importantly, we would talk about life. During these conversations, I learned Louis was an avid skier which gave us a great deal to talk about. Other times he stopped in for advice on a product idea he was working on, chats about family, and a possible move to Tennessee.

The next class that Louis and I worked together was BADM 280, International & Intercultural Business. This course was a late sprint course online with a three-week lab in Italy. Where do I even begin to tell of the adventures we had together?

I guess it started with the trip to the airport, Louis, the other students and I navigating our way through security at the airport. Next, after a long flight and a change of planes, we were in Italy; Venice to be more precise. I will never forget Louis' face when we were on the waterbus from the airport to our B & B and the reality of the long journey we had just made set in. This was a whole new experience for Louis as it was his first time away from his family.

I have to admit that I feel very honored that his first trip away was with me and other students. The first week in Venice was filled with tours and shopping excursions as well as project work. One of my favorite tours was of San Marco Square and the Palace. Due to the fact that Louis was in his wheelchair, he and I were able to go places in the Palace that others were not permitted. That was fascinating to me to be able to see parts of the Palace that were closed to most of the general public.

The next week was spent in the Alps. We went eyeglass shopping and toured the Olympic Ski Jump. The tour of the jump helped prove to us that Louis' wheelchair was capable of being "off road". LOL. At one point myself and another student strapped on rollerblades and took Louis from Italy to Austria on a bike trail. Louis went to the top of mountains with us; to scenic overlooks; back to the eyeglass shop and in a paddle boat just to give a brief overview of our Alps adventures. Back to Venice for more tours.

The last week in Venice was filled with more adventures. We went to San Giorgio tower, a beach barbeque (again proving the four-wheel drive capabilities of Louis' wheelchair), the navigation tower for ships, a tour of the boat Arsenal and a ride in a Gondola. I know that there are so many things that I am neglecting to mention that we did on this trip. Also, come to think of it, it wasn't necessarily the adventures that I remember as much as being a part of my students' life for every waking moment for twenty-two days.

On this trip, students get to experience things that they may only do once in a lifetime but it is the day in and day out living that really makes me feel lucky to share this experience with them. If I was to tell you that Louis made the experience different – I would be very honest in telling you that and when I say different, I simply mean a different experience for the other students and for me. Why was it different? Because Louis being there made me see the world more through his eyes than I had ever experienced before.

At one point I was helping Louis after a shower and I grabbed his glasses and held them up and said to him, "Wow. These glasses are awfully dirty. Could you even see Venice today?" That brought a laughter out of Louis that I had never heard before, a real hardy chuckle is how I would classify it. This told me that Louis had totally let his guard down and was truly enjoying this experience as much as I was. Next, we had to head home. We did not have the smoothest of journeys home but we made it with a few minor hassles. As we arrived home I could see the joy in Louis' face when he saw his family and I took a moment to reflect on what a great experience I had on this trip because Louis was there.

The lessons that I have learned from this student are countless and amazing. Deep down, I know Louis will make it back to Italy one day with his family and at that point, Louis will connect with the network of lives that he touched while in Italy. Most of the emails that I receive from my Italian coworkers now often ask about Louis and how he is and when will he return to Italy.

Ode di Luigi

Louis that was quite a trip we took,

It was nice to learn without the use of a book,

And those Italians sure know how to cook.

Remember the outside restaurant where we would dine?

The pasta Bolognese and the sampling of wine,

the breeze from the Adriatic Sea — life was just fine!

How about the tour of the grand Lido hotel?

When I was pushing you up the ramp I almost fell,

I think it was a rock in your tire or maybe a shell?

As I remember, San Giorgio tower was a great day I think.

That was a day when the whole group was in sync.

Also, the night of the sunset when the sky was so pink.

Then the Alps and the mountains and the ski jump hike,

us with rollerblades and a four-wheeler while the others rode a bike.

And Alberto with his fishing stories about catching that giant pike.

Louis, I know you of all people love Italy as much as I do,

so I think if I were you I would take that as a cue,

to go with your family one day and show them "the Italy you."

I have met a great number of students over the years,

Some I have lost unfortunately and for those there were tears,

And the most satisfying is when you help students with their fears.

I may not have helped with your fears, but I did see you grow.

In ways that make me proud that you are a person I know.

Now it is time to take that growth and use it wherever you go.

You are certainly a student I will remember with a thought and a smile.

A guy with a sense of humor, an interesting thought and a sense of style.

A person that would give you the shirt off his back and go the extra mile.

So, HVCC bids you farewell as a grad and views you as a friend.

And as you travel we will hope to see you around the next bend.

We all here at HVCC want to see you again so this is not THE END.

So, that is a tough course to follow but Louis took his last class with me online. The course was BADM 208, Organizational Leadership, and his performance in that course earned him an "A". Come to think of it, Louis received an "A" in all of the courses that he took with me as his instructor. Through the BADM 208 course, I learned even more about Louis. This learning experience was different for me because this time I learned more about Louis' ability to write and put his thoughts on paper.

I know in the teaching profession we see a great number of students come and go, but there are some students that you want to succeed and at the same time have a tough time saying goodbye to them. Is Louis a friend? Yes, and a very good one that I hope keeps in touch. Also, Louis and I will be going skiing this season, I am just waiting for him to arrange a date to do so with me. Maybe February 22? If that happens, I will have another adventure to share with you. Yes, another chapter in the book of Louis Vendetti!

AFTERWORD

by Dr. Valerie Lang Waldin, J.D., M.L.S.,
Associate Professor/Librarian

When I was a student at Skidmore in 1982, I remember an exercise in a psychology class. The activity involved looking at another person and thinking of *one* word to most accurately describe that person. We all do that to some extent, whether we are aware of it or not.

Looking at Louis, one sees the obvious: a young man in a wheelchair. Disabled? Impaired? Fragile? Working with Louis, a different vision emerges.

My affiliation with Louis came at a time when my husband was diagnosed with stage four inoperable lung cancer. The human body he took for granted was slipping away. My view of the nature of successful living was forever altered. About this time, I started to assist Louis with intensive, sophisticated entrepreneurial research. The entrepreneurship course of study at Hudson Valley Community College is rigorous, demanding and rewarding; though proves too ambitious for some. Not Louis.

I recall looking at Louis as he plowed through his profoundly challenging entrepreneurship assignments, planned his time to the hour, and bravely confronted every day with a leap of faith. Whether he knows it or not, Louis helped to teach me humility, faith, and persistence in the face of overpowering adversity. Each time I was in Louis' presence, I felt a simple goodness and light the world seems so desperate for. He not only impacted me: colleagues and students slowed down, became gentler, and more compassionate. His great intellect overshadowed any physical disability. His integrity eclipsed gratuities. His courage served as a model for the most gifted of students. Louis fostered the change we strive to see, and his commencement from Hudson Valley Community College was just that; a beginning of wondrous contributions to all who cross his path.

I began this afterword by describing a psychology exercise in college requiring our class to use one word to describe a fellow classmate. When you read this quote by Calvin Coolidge, our nation's 30th president, you will know the one word, above all, that describes Louis.

> *Nothing in this world can take the place of persistence. Talent will not: nothing is more common than unsuccessful men with talent. Genius will not; unrewarded genius is almost a proverb. Education will not: the world is full of educated derelicts. Persistence and determination alone are omnipotent.*

Lou is talented, a genius in my judgment, and definitely educated. But most importantly, he is *persistent. Think about that.* In my opinion, persistence is the best quality a human being can have. And Lou exudes persistence every minute of every day of his life.

This book is a gift of insight of a life honorably lived, timeless values, and the daily honor of being alive. Thank you, Louis.

Paul Moylan

November 29, 1955 – April 13, 2018

When I found out about Paul Moylan's death, I was stunned; I didn't know what to think, much less what to do. The Wednesday before, he was publicizing the fact that he was going to be at my local American Legion Post to sing with a band called Katsura. The band was originally supposed to play a few weeks earlier, but the performance was postponed until April 13, 2018. Little did I know, that was the last night that he was going to be with me on this earth.

As I talked about in chapter one: "My Elementary School Years," I had an Individualized Education Plan (IEP) that dictated that I would have a one-on-one aide who would be in my classes. In chapter two, "My Middle School Years," I talked about how my IEP was changed; how I would no longer have a one-on-one aide, but "access to an aide" (which, in middle school, meant that the aide was assigned to a group of students; as I got older, it meant that I only had an aide for transitions from class to class, and in Physical Education — because of the physically demanding nature of the class).

One of the things that I liked about Mr. Moylan is that he was always full of love for his fellow man. He had a wonderful sense of humor; he knew when it was time for fun and games, but also when things had to be taken seriously.

One example of this that comes to mind was when it came to fire drills. One time, the fire alarm went off when we were headed to the elevator from the second floor of the high school to get back to the first floor so I could go to my next class of the day. I only had about five to ten minutes to accomplish this task, so I had to move rather quickly. As we were headed to the elevator, we were talking and laughing about various things. When the fire alarm went off, though, we immediately went into what we called my "fire drill protocol," which was attempting to get down the stairs as quickly as possible, while maintaining safety.

We did this the one time, though, and realized that it wasn't an ideal situation. So, we worked together to come up with a plan of how I was going to deal with fire drills, which was when I was on the first floor, I would go outside with everyone else; if I was on the second floor, I would go to the nearest stairwell and stay there for the duration of it.

I also remember another time when I was in Spanish class and the fire alarm went off, but Mr. Moylan wasn't able to get to me in time to start getting out before the bell went off (as was our normal procedure so I wasn't caught in the stream of students and faculty attempting to get out of the building). Luckily, my Spanish class was on the first floor and rather close to an exit, so I was able to get out quickly, despite having to navigate around the other students.

When we met back in 2008, I was a scared sixth-grader just going into Bethlehem Central Middle School (understandably scared because it was relatively bigger than Elsmere Elementary School, where I had been for the five years prior; not to mention the fact that I got lost while on the tour of the middle school)!

Mr. Moylan saw this scared sixth-grade student, and he helped me out tremendously to get acquainted with the layout of the school and the best ways to go to get to my classes (although, sometimes, there was only one way—which was awesome so I couldn't get lost!).

When I was going to class and didn't remember which way to go, he would guide me there (although, it only took me a few weeks to make a map of the entire school in my head, no matter if it be the middle school or high school) and then I was set; sometimes even getting to my class faster than Mr. Moylan because I "ran" and took "shortcuts"! But sometimes I was just fast so I could either have time to visit the secretaries in the main office or with my teacher for the upcoming class before the class began, as I always loved to visit with them.

While in high school, Mr. Moylan saw me accomplish great things: Like dancing to the steps on the music in my senior Ballroom dancing class in high school. Because I couldn't dance with a partner with the other students, I danced on a mat off to the side within the gymnasium. Despite this, I still danced; I just used my crutches and moved slowly through the dance to make sure that I got the steps correct.

This happened the first few days of the dance, but after I started to get the steps down, I would speed up a bit. I got proficient enough at one of the dances where I was able to dance to the beat of the music and, as if on cue, turn and do the dance again; doing that around the mat until I came back to where I was standing, facing forward once again.

Mr. Moylan also went with me to B.O.C.E.S., as they were unable to supply a one-on-one aide for me; they said that the district had to send one.

When I was in B.O.C.E.S., as Mr. Moylan talked about in "My Travels with Lou," I had to pretty much teach myself the coursework while attending this school. That, along with the fact that one student in the first class moved faster through it then a majority of us, put tons of stress on me (or, maybe, I put undue stress upon myself for it, who knows?).

The (undue) stress that I put on myself was manifesting in ways that I didn't even know were possible: I would get physically ill; I would have a stomach ache; and, twice, I would break down and cry. Once when that happened, I told Mr. Moylan that I wanted to go for a walk; luckily, he could tell that there was something more to it than that. The second time that this occurred, I broke down while in the classroom — which was embarrassing.

When we went outside, I was already bawling my eyes out; crying so much to the point I couldn't breathe. I couldn't calm myself down enough to speak. The tears just kept coming. After a few minutes of crying, the tears stopped; that was the point when Mr. Moylan started talking to me, trying to figure out what happened.

Mr. Moylan was also with me during the College in the High School course that I took on their campus with Hudson Valley Community College. He wrote in his piece, "When Lou was a senior at B.O.C.E.S. he got his first taste of a college business course, with college credit attached! He excelled in it and his future direction began to take shape." When I was given the syllabus, I looked it over to see what was in the course. It looked to be an interesting and fun course with videos of current entrepreneurs like Brian Scudamore of 1-800-GOT-JUNK?®, but I didn't like the fact that we had various presentations throughout the semester; I hated public speaking with a passion —

now, I just tolerate it; sometimes I look forward to it, but it's *not* my favorite thing to do.

In the last piece of the above quote, Mr. Moylan says, ". . . He excelled in it and his future direction began to take shape." At the time of taking the course, I was on track to go to Hudson Valley in their Computer Information Systems degree program.

After taking this course, I was "hooked," and wanted to learn more about this, as I knew deep down that it would help me fulfill my lifelong dream of owning my own business. At the end of the school year, I visited the college's Admissions Office and changed my major from Computer Information Systems to Entrepreneurship and I never looked back.

Mr. Moylan was gracious even to stay in contact with me even after high school, which was a great blessing to me.

After I graduated high school on June 26, 2015, Mr. Moylan and I stayed in contact via Facebook, where we talked about various things from my time in college, to how my sister was doing in school, to a recent conversation that we had where he said that the problems he was having with his foot were back and that they may cause him to retire early.

Even though I wasn't in Bethlehem any longer, Mr. Moylan showed the same love and caring nature toward me in our interactions. He encouraged me to keep going with my degree when it was tough to do; he checked in with me about my sister, Loren, too, as he worked with her on occasion.

A day or two after his passing, I wrote a small tribute to him on my Facebook page. I received many wonderful comments from friends offering their condolences, but there were a few that stuck out to me.

One was from a friend of mine named Paula in which she said, "I do not like when human relationships of such huge magnitude are reduced to titles. The relationship between a person who needs assistance and a human that becomes that help is a kinship of love and trust. . . ."

Another was from one of Mr. Moylan's relatives named Susan, in which she said, ". . . I would like to share with you, however, that he didn't take a piece of you when he left. Rather, he left a piece of himself with you so that you might do great things. . ."

We certainly did have a bond, an unbreakable bond, forged over ten years. He helped me and supported me through my schooling. When times had gotten tough; he helped me through my challenges, to triumph; to come out the other side a stronger person.

"I'm not handicapped; I'm handi-capable!"

One thing that Mr. Moylan talked to me about over the years was the fact that my disability didn't define who I was. He also had his own challenges growing up (like his vision, which caused him to wear glasses). Despite his vision problems, though, he didn't think of himself as "visually impaired" or "handicapped"; he thought of himself as "handi-capable." He talked to me about one quote when I was young, and then it was brought up again at his wake when I was talking to his sister, Susan, "I'm not handicapped; I'm handi-capable!" It is how he lived his life: He believed and had the confidence in himself that he was capable of doing many great things despite his vision problems. He was a musician; he helped alongside his wife, in a jail, teaching inmates skills they would need if they ever went back into society, among other things.

. . . .

I will forever be grateful for the times that we shared together, the lessons that he has taught me, and the many wonderful memories of the fun times and lessons, as well as of him as a person, that he left with me.

Rest in Peace, Mr. Moylan. You will be forever missed; not only by me, but by all of the people whom you touched with your selfless, giving nature over the years.

ACKNOWLEDGMENTS

To Dr. Andrew J. "Drew" Matonak, Ed.D., for taking the time out of your busy schedule to write the Foreword for this book. Thank you also for your thirteen years of leadership to the college. It is greatly appreciated by many.

To Dr. Valerie Lang Waldin, J.D., M.L.S., Associate Professor/Librarian for writing the Afterword for this book, and for everything that you have done for me throughout my time at Hudson Valley. Your guidance has helped me earn A's on the most important projects of my college career. Without you, that wouldn't be possible.

To Jodi Mather for the inspiration to change my major from Computer Information Systems to Entrepreneurship. You reignited in me the drive, the desire to start my own business.

To Doreen McGreevy for helping me when my studies had become overwhelming. Thank you for helping me become organized and successfully complete them each semester.

To Andrew F. Roberts for helping me make sure that my papers made sense when read.

To Marlo Daniels for helping me get through my English Composition I research paper. Without you, I would still be writing it today.

To Sushmita Chatterji for helping me manage my nervousness for Public Speaking. Now, I feel that I have a better grasp on how to go about dealing with my anxiety when it comes to public speaking, and how to effectively write and deliver a speech.

To the staff of the Center for Access and Assistive Technology at Hudson Valley Community College. Thank you for all that you have done to help me through my classes and to earn my degree.

To my mom and dad. Thank you for all that you have done and continue to do for me. Without your continued guidance, support, and love; I would not be where I am today. Special thanks to my dad for always driving me where I needed to go.

To my sister, for all of her help through the years. It was nice to know she was never too far away throughout our school years. Although, yes, I know that siblings can fight, I know that she always has my back, as I do hers.

To Cindi Hamel for all of your help through B.O.C.E.S. and beyond. Thank you for helping me get back in line when I strayed. Thank you for always being there for me when I needed someone to listen. Thank you for encouraging me to go for my dreams.

To the following people for taking the time out of your schedules to write pieces for this book. It's greatly appreciated!

- Dr. Andrew J. "Drew" Matonak, Ed.D., President, Hudson Valley Community College

- Karen Vendetti

- Karen Anthony

- Paul Moylan

- Wayne Sharp

- Tanya Fredricks, Clerk, Center for Academic Engagement, Hudson Valley Community College

- Ricky P. Thibodeau, Department Chair, Accounting, Entrepreneurship and Marketing; Director, School of Business Advisement Center; Faculty, School of Business

- Theresa and Ron Craig, Sean Craig's parents

- Andrew F. Roberts, Site Supervisor and Academic Coach, Center for Academic Engagement, Hudson Valley Community College

- John Meehan, Associate Professor, Business Administration, Hudson Valley Community College

- Dr. Valerie Lang Waldin, J.D., M.L.S., Associate Professor/Librarian

To Eric Van Der Hope for your continued support throughout the writing process. Without you, this book would not be what it is today.

Without you, this book wouldn't even be in the hands of readers—thank you for helping me streamline the finishing of this book and getting me back on track!

Thank you *all* for all of your help, love, and support throughout the years, supporting my dreams, and the publication of this book.

NOTES

1. "Rotary Scout Reservation." *Facebook*, www.facebook.com/pg/RSRBSA/about.

2. "Advancement and Awards." *Boy Scouts of America*, Boy Scouts of America, www.scouting.org/Home/BoyScouts/Advance mentandAwards.aspx.

3. Gary G. Schoeniger, Clifton L. Taulbert. "Who Owns the Ice House?: Eight Life Lessons from an Unlikely Entrepreneur EBook: Gary G. Schoeniger, Clifton L. Taulbert: Kindle Store." Amazon.com: Who Owns the Ice House?: Eight Life Lessons from an Unlikely Entrepreneur EBook: Gary G. Schoeniger, Clifton L. Taulbert: Kindle Store, 29 Apr. 2015, www.amazon.com/Who-Owns-Ice-House-Entrepreneur-ebook/dp/B00WUTVUHG.

4. "Policies and Procedures." *Policies and Procedures - Hudson Valley Community College - Acalog ACMS™*, catalog.hvcc.edu/content.php?catoid=2&navoid=55.

5. "An Oversaturated Market 2014." *Funeral Consumers Alliance*, 7 May 2014, funerals.org/too-many-funeral-homes-2014.

6. Ibid.

7. "Pepsi Next." *Wikipedia*, Wikimedia Foundation, 25 Dec. 2017, en.wikipedia.org/wiki/Pepsi_Next.

8. "Entrepreneurship, A.A.S." *Program: Entrepreneurship, A.A.S. - Hudson Valley Community College - Acalog ACMS™*, catalog.hvcc.edu/preview_program.php?catoid=2andpoid=125.

9. "What Is Green Burial?" *Green Burial Council*, greenburialcouncil.org/home/what-is-green-burial.

Made in the
USA
Middletown, DE